SOLO-OPS

SOLO-OPS

A Survival Guide for
Military Wives

Hilary Martin

To order additional copies of this book, contact:
Xlibris Corporation
1-888-795-4274
www.Xlibris.com
Orders@Xlibris.com
17211

CONTENTS

PROLOGUE

The Importance of Humor

When my mother joined the Army, her assigned duty station was Honolulu, Hawaii. Before arriving there, she was required to go to a mandatory finance class. The name of the class is pretty descriptive and it was obvious that the Army wanted her to be able to understand Army financing.

Everyone was reluctant to be there. The class was scheduled to be four hours long, and I can imagine the weariness and disdain. It seems that when you join the military, they begin treating you like a child. I guess it is true what they say: "There is the right way . . . and then, there is the Army way."

The teacher stood at the front of the crowded, weary class and said, "My job is to talk to you about Army finances. I realize that when you walk out of this classroom, you won't remember a thing I have said about finance. You will probably just have a serious case of 'dead ass'.

"I am giving this lecture because, one, it's required, and two, because OBC [Officers Basic Course] is not really teaching about the Army. It's only going to teach you the necessity of developing a sense of humor. If you don't develop a sense of humor in the military, you won't survive." He then continued with his finance lecture for the remainder of the four hours.

As predicted, nearly 20 years later, my mother has forgotten the name of the man who spoke that day. She has forgotten every word of his finance lecture, and can only vaguely remember being lectured at all. But she does remember his preliminary comments quite clearly, because they were so true.

She still tells me this story often whenever I am having trouble with the military. Maybe, it was not because of this man that my mother developed her sense of humor, but she did heed his warning well. She developed a fabulous sense of humor, and has survived and continued to survive through 10 years in the military—and 10 years after getting out. Today, she still works in a military hospital, and she still laughs at the Army.

I think, as wives, we are required to develop the same sense of humor. We have even less control over things than our husbands do. I have learned that when the military hands you lemons, smile and laugh about it later with your friends. The military is a very silly and often ridiculous institution. While it is easy to find blame or be upset, neither of these maneuvers help you to cope. It is more productive to find a good laugh, shake your head, and not take anything too seriously.

I hope to persuade you of the value of laughing at yourself and help you learn not to take life too seriously. Laughter will make even the worst things a little easier to survive. I trust that you do intend to survive.

CHAPTER 1

Welcome to the Military

Now, WAKE UP!

So your significant other has joined the military. Congratulations, and good luck in staying sane. You are in for the ride of your life, and that can make anyone a little crazy. Whether you are a girlfriend, fiancée, or a wife, the time has come for you to make a difficult life choice that many give little thought to.

A number of wives contend that they have nothing to do with the military because they are not in it. They refuse to be involved in any classes, briefings or activities affiliated with the military. Then they continue to whine and complain because they can't understand what is going on with their SO (Significant Other). When I come across a wife like this, I have no sympathy; few veteran wives do.

This is as good a time as any to wake up and examine your life and yourself. If you don't believe these things, it's all going to be uphill from here, baby. I really must wish you luck, because, y'know, you're going to need it!

I'll tell you right now that the military does not qualify as merely a job; it is a lifestyle. Even though you will not be actively involved in your SO's job, you will be actively dealing with the military way of life. So, in that sense, you *are* in the military.

Although you do not wear rank, you will endure long separations from your husband, receive treatment in military facilities, and make homes in places that are foreign to you. Choosing to marry your SO is an implied agreement to join the military.

Always keep this in mind during the times of hardship which you will undoubtedly encounter throughout your husband's career: Remember, this is not just his choice; it is also *your* choice, so best to deal with it like an adult.

You have a "part-time" husband. If you are not yet married or he has not yet "signed his life away," you must decide before you marry whether you wish to deal with this or not. You will no longer be the only "cherry on his sundae." He is married to the military first, and family often takes the back seat.

Many women question their own ability to function without a man in their lives. This is sad. I assure you that all women have this ability, but many fail to make the choice. Many military wives continue to be co-dependents by choice, much to the annoyance of the rest of us.

The military will challenge the strength of your love and commitment to each other, and there will be some heinous fights along the way. Resolving conflict is the stuff that marriage is made of, after all. In the end, if you have not yet parted, you will be that much stronger.

After accepting the fact that you yourself have also chosen this lifestyle, the way to survive it is to embrace it, the good as well as the bad! Somewhat like you embracing your husband even when he smells like old feet. (If your husband has never smelled like old feet, you have even more of the joys of military life to experience ahead.)

Don't make the mistake of focusing merely on the negative aspects and overlooking the advantages that come with being a military wife. Do whatever is needed to overcome feelings of doubt and concern, and face your new life with optimism and excitement! Feel about the military the same as how you feel about your husband because now, they are one and the same. (But please remember, everyone hates her husband sometimes. It's only normal.)

As a wife, you now have a daunting task in front of you. It is your responsibility to function as the head of the household (no matter what your husband may think). You are his support system and **your attitude will directly affect his success.** The journey on which you are about to embark is whatever you make of it. Decide now whether the next 4-30 years of your life will be joyful . . . or miserable. The military cannot make you unhappy. Happiness is a personal choice and it's one of the few things the military will allow you to choose.

The military is, for all purposes, a very flawed organization. People in the military can help make it a more enjoyable experience. Your future neighbors, friends, and acquaintances all await you at your undisclosed future duty station. These awesome people, coupled with a good attitude and some patience on your side, will make military life worthwhile.

The most important aspect of surviving military life is having a sense of humor. Have I said that yet? The ability to laugh at your own expense is priceless during times of hardships, and wonderful during good times. You will face many challenges; you will lose many battles. Okay, maybe every battle. The government is not big on losing (if you haven't noticed) and they do not change their policies for mere service members' wives. Heck, they don't change for anyone.

My mother always enjoyed the television show *MASH* before she joined the Army, but she assumed that things must be dramatically exaggerated. After she joined, she realized that the adventures of the 4077th were actually toned down compared to the real thing.

MASH is a great example of military humor. These people were faced with the dire conditions of war. They lived in tents, used latrines, and made due with dwindling supplies. In addition, they faced the stress of watching servicemen die on a daily basis in the hospital, and being separated from their families. Not to mention experiencing personal fear of death from the war.

Despite all the reasons they had to feel unhappy, the 4077th personnel could still have a good laugh at the Army's, and their own, expense at the end of the day. They set a great example for all of us. I believe that if these people can be happy while in the midst of war, we can be happy in the midst of everyday service life.

By buying this book, you have already taken the first step in making the most of your circumstances. Whatever your family's reason was for joining the military, I hope that I can help you make a smoother transition into your new lifestyle, because now you are also a part of *my* family.

I have attempted to give you a glance at what military life is really like and discuss the challenges that you will be facing in your husband's new career. I write from personal experience and want to share my lessons with you. My comments about the military may seem shocking, but I can assure you that you will discover that they are (for the most part) true.

The Military "Facilitating Family" (Total Oxymoron)

One of the first things you might hear about the military is their recent changes regarding family members. In my many years of experience, I have noted that the military does nothing purely for the well-being of its servicemen. The motives for these so-called changes seem superficial and self-serving.

However, if a change is for the good of the families, I question its value. Always be skeptical when the military is trying to help you out "just to be nice." This does not happen and if it seems to, there is always an organizational motive behind it. The military often offers little more than just "lip service."

Their policies (also known as their lips) say that they won't move you around as much as they may have in the past. Keep in mind, this does not mean you won't be moving. If they feel like it, they will make an exception to their own policy—over and over, if need be. Not moving as much can be a good thing if you are happy at your initial station, but it can be misery if you are sent to a place you hate.

I can tell you right off the bat that *most* people dislike their current duty stations. Nothing can ever quite compare to home. It is really hard to resist missing where you were and comparing it unfavorably to where you are. This is a popular military sport.

I suspect that this stated change (for our benefit) has come about so that they can save money by moving people around less.

Be advised, if you hate your current station, you won't be going anywhere for a while. Conversely, if you love your new home, you should expect to be moved soon. The military does not tolerate happiness for long periods of time; it's bad for their morale. The military "fun police" must be kept busy.

According to the military, TRICARE (military health insurance) is also more user friendly and easier to understand. Right. Give them a call-up and ask them anything to test how user friendly they are. I avoid confrontations with TRICARE at all costs.

If you ever hear the words "TRICARE" and "friendly" used in the same sentence, just know that you are being misled. TRICARE has never seemed to care, nor have I ever found them friendly. The military may fool itself about these things, but you would do well to expect from TRICARE what you expect from *any* insurance company. To sum it up: "They TRY to care."

"The command has an open-door policy and is ready to deal with potential family problems more effectively." More effectively than what? If you know anything about the military, you may already be stricken with the urge to laugh, but this is the official policy.

To continue: "The military provides more day care facilities, marriage counseling and other family services.

"Housing is more readily available and the BAH (Basic Allowance for Housing) is more appropriate than in the past." Note that more appropriate is not the same as *is* appropriate.

"The military no longer discourages marriage, but rather, supports it." Are you seeing any discrepancies here?

Hey! The government has finally seen the light! They have conducted official studies to find out why servicemen don't re-enlist. They have discovered that wives (in particular) do not enjoy being treated as a mere inconvenience. Women do not usually enjoy giving birth to babies, attending funerals, and taking care of other important family events alone.

Wives do not enjoy lengthy unaccompanied tours or being treated as a pain in the ass when conducting business on the base. They do not enjoy their husbands being paid peanuts, their families living in substandard housing, all the while watching their tired men return home from another exhausting day.

.They take issue with being constantly ignored and uninformed about important events concerning their loved one. They despise the endless shuffling around, quitting jobs and leaving friends, only to do it again at the next station.

They find it hard to appreciate a military that treats them as an unnecessary luxury, so they oppose their husbands' re-enlisting! Well, DUH! I wonder how much they paid the genius who conducted this study? I could have given that answer free of charge.

Well, now that they have found the problem, have they fixed it? *They say* it is 100 percent better. While the government seems to be mighty proud of this, I find myself questioning the entire campaign. Many civilians have bought it. But every day, I meet women who are dealing with the same issues that wives have been dealing with for years. Maybe the military has come a long way. Even so, there is still a long way to go before these problems will be remedied.

I actually question whether the nature of military service allows for this kind of change at all. Now that they have deluded themselves into believing that they have fixed the problem, I fear that they have stopped working on it. This alone should tell you that wives take no priority. They have worked on improving helicopters longer than they have worked on this!

Despite what the military hierarchy may say (and they will say a lot of things over the years), you are another problem in somebody's day and another stack of papers on somebody's desk. For truly, if they had "wanted your husband to have a wife, they would have issued him one."

You will be avoided by the command, hindered from carrying out important business because you do not have Power of Attorney (or the *right* Power of Attorney), and set aside for not doing active duty yourself. It is these things that can drive a wife to hate the military, everyone in it, and (in some cases) her husband for joining it.

This is why you must endure everything with a sense of humor. The choice comes down to hatred or humor. Few people actually enjoy a life based on hatred. In time, you can find your own way to keep yourself sane. Service life is something that you need to adapt to and, over time, you will. Whether you believe it or not.

The military has not, is not, and will not be "family friendly" for a long time. This is something we wives need to deal with. Forget all the hype you have heard regarding the military, because it's probable that you have been misinformed.

I find that this is often the case, so I have prepared a list of things that you would benefit from knowing in order to deal with the military effectively. These are the inalienable truths, and you will find that they are exactly what you need to know.

The 20 Inalienable Truths about the Military

The following inalienable truths will be expanded on in the chapters that follow:

1. The recruiter lied to you. (Ch. 1)
2. The military just loves paperwork. (Ch. 2)
3. You will not "make good money." (Ch. 3)
4. The U.S. Constitution does not apply to your husband. (Ch. 4)
5. There is nothing "free" in the military. (Ch.5)
6. The military reserves the right not to pay you. (Ch. 5)
7. The military understands the meaning of the word "policy." (Ch. 5)
8. If you think the military gave you a good deal, you've still got your surprise coming. (Ch. 6)
9. You will not be "seeing the world." (Ch. 6)
10. Someone is always to blame in the military. (Ch. 6)
11. You will not "pick" your duty station. (Ch. 7)
12. Try not to acquire anything that does not travel well. (Ch. 7)
13. You are moving to the ghetto. (Ch. 8)
14. Uniformity is crucial. (Ch. 8)
15. There is no such thing as a good duty station or post. (Ch. 8)
16. Ceremony is more important than life itself. (Ch. 9)

17. An "estimated date of arrival" is a joke. (Ch. 10)
18. The military loves to get involved. (Ch. 11)
19. Nothing will ever be taken care of in a "quick and timely" fashion. (Ch. 11)
20. Expect the unexpected. (Ch. 12)
21. (An afterthought) The military is the military. (Ch. 12)

How the Government REALLY Is

Most civilians live their entire lives blissfully ignorant of the adventures of military life. They seem to believe that the government has got it all together and that they are perfectly safe.

In close association with the military, it takes only a short time to convince any civilian (including yourself) that this is far from the truth. Not many people understand the U.S. government as well as the men and women in the military. You, as a wife, will also come to understand many things that you were oblivious to as a civilian.

In order to function well in a military family, you have to develop a certain attitude about the government and its policies. The way I look at it, you either need to hate them, or you need to understand and accept why they act as they do.

I have met many women who seem to understand the government, accept their policies, programs and propaganda, all the while entertaining the belief that there is some logical reason behind it. These ladies say things like "The country is more important than me having my husband around while I give birth. I'm not that selfish."

While this might be easy to say, it is not easy to believe, particularly if you are a pregnant and emotional woman who is about to give birth. I have never been able to see how it benefits the military or the country to alienate a wife in the name of training.

I cannot begin to understand why the government treats people so badly. My choice has always been to ridicule them. After all, I do not care *why* my husband cannot be around for a few hours while I give birth; I only care that he is not around to begin with.

I see no excuse for him *not* to be there, unless of course, he is in the process of single-handedly strangling Osama himself. In that case, I might excuse him. Other than that, there are many other men who can take his place while he attends an event so important to us.

The military, in fact, is completely irrational and contradicts itself frequently. It acts similar to the looniest mental patient you have ever met. I have learned to expect nothing from the government but more problems, and (at the best) nothing at all. I think you should, too.

This way, when something happens that seems to completely destroy your entire life, you won't be too surprised about it. In not having to deal with the surprise of the situation, you will be able to handle it more competently. Also, it is a working attitude in general because you can save your surprise for when they actually do something *helpful*. It will make the triumph and pleasure of that much greater for you. Is this cynical? Oh, yes.

Cynicism allows you to vent your frustrations about the military more frequently. I do not condone calling your husband's command to yell about how the military affects your personal situation. In truth, they don't care, and this maneuver does not help his career. It also makes you look bad. I do, however, think you have the right and even the obligation to bitch at anyone else who'll listen about it.

This is your country as much as it is anyone else's. The First Amendment gives civilians the right to complain, and you are a civilian. So gripe away. Your husband is defending your right to do so. You can't let him think that you don't appreciate your rights and his contribution. Just don't allow it to consume you with grief. It's supposed to be helpful—not hurtful.

Some might try and convince you that you should not complain because the military doesn't like it. That is a fine rule for your husband. He is not supposed to complain because the government is his boss, and he can get in trouble for it (see truth #4).

However, you are a civilian (although the military might like you to feel otherwise) and *you* still have civil rights. If the military doesn't like it, that's their problem. They obviously don't care about *your* problems (giving birth alone) so why should you be overly concerned with theirs?

Don't ever let anyone talk you out of your "make fun of the military" therapy. Laughter is the best medicine, and if the medicine comes at the government's expense, it's even better.

Playing Chess with Uncle Sam

Being in the military is a game of strategy. Some people are unaware of this and find themselves shocked when they end up on the losing side of a military-vs.-me situation. Both parties are trying to get the maximum amount of benefits from the other, with a minimum of sacrifices.

The difference between you and the military is that the military has had extensive war training. Unfortunately, they do not offer this training to wives. I guess that would be bad for their strategy.

The game goes like this: Your husband does not want to be deployed or be stationed in Wichita, Kansas. He just wants to support his family or have the chance to go to college.

The government does not want to pay for his medical expenses or his college; they just want another mindless drone to follow orders and die for them, if necessary. The benefits are the incentives to play. In play, if you watch your back and know the rules, you can usually get out relatively unscathed. But you have to learn the game and the various rules by which you can ensure your "win."

You must remember that the military's only goal is to come out on top—it is a self-serving organization. They will win in the end, no matter what. The object of *your* game is to make sure that it is a win-win game, rather than a win-lose game in favor of the military. Those are your only options.

You need to be sure that you take advantage of the military, as they are sure to take advantage of you. The military helps the military first. The military helps you only when you convince them that it helps *them* to help you.

But Our Recruiter Told Us . . .

If I had a dime for each time a man or woman had uttered this phrase, I wouldn't need to live on my husband's paltry salary. If you believe anything that I have written up to this point, you have already realized that the recruiter may not have been completely truthful. A recruiter has only the capabilities to make the military look good. That is his job, and if he wasn't good at it, he wouldn't be doing it. Although it is sad, it is also true.

Truth #1: *The Recruiter lied to you.* I'm sure when your husband got to boot camp, the DI (drill instructor) told him enough times that the recruiter was full of lies. Too bad, he is already in. There is no amount of bitching that you can do now that will change this horrible, yet true, fact. You will just have to suffer, like everyone else who has ever believed a recruiter. Here is a head's up! If you are still under the impression that you got a good deal from the recruiter, just wait. I'm sure this irrational feeling of yours will not last for the *entire* four years.

My Suggestions for More Appropriate Recruiting Slogans
(Not quite as catchy, but appropriate nonetheless)

"Even Though We Have Malaria, We Still Police the Area."

"Do You Like Showering with Men? Join the Navy!"

"The Clean-Shaven Few, the Proud, the Marines."

"You Will Learn Something from Being Punished for Your Co-Workers' Mistakes!"

"Learn How to Live on a Budget, Join the Army!"

"Air Force: It's Good Enough, for Government Work!"

"You Don't Know the Rush of Endangering Your Life Until You've Been to Kuwait."

"See the World . . . Just Kidding, See Ft. Hood!"

"Test Your Marriage, Join the Marines."

"We Came, We Saw, We Pitched a Tent and Got Scabies."

"Find out How Organized the Government Isn't."

"Join the Navy to See All the Whorehouses in the World!"
"Learn about Respect. Or Just Learn How to Do 500
Pushups in an Hour."
"We'll Make a Man Out of You: With Sleep Deprivation."
"Army of One. But If One Man Can Do It All, What
Would You Need the Rest of Us For?"
"Do You Hate Your Wife? Join the Navy!"
"Hurry up and Wait, Except at the Recruiter's Office."

Your Initiation

When your husband is promoted, you will feel pride for him
that is almost unreal. Promotions are a big deal in the military,
and you will learn that. You will watch your husband work hard
and struggle with various things during his career, all the while,
feeling helpless to assist him in anything.

When he is finally rewarded for all of his efforts, you will feel
as if things are finally going his way. The feeling is pure joy and he
might as well be the president as far as you are concerned. And the
extra five dollars a month is great, too . . .

A curious ritual in the military is the "pinning on" ceremony,
also known as a "blood pinning." You might notice large holes in
his chest after a promotion ceremony. Even though he may have
truly earned his rank, others will feel the need to haze (initiate)
him. When they pin his new rank on his collar they do not bother
to put the backings on, because it would require far too much
effort on the part of the pin-on guy, whoever he may be.

After the ceremony, the other men will run up and smack him
in the chest, driving the pins straight into his flesh. If this does not
occur, they can always beat the ever-loving shit out of him, or
perform half a dozen other rituals that you will, no doubt, find
barbaric.

I hope to God that I never have to witness this in person. I
have seen the scars on my husband's chest, and he has come home
bleeding over and over again. I've decided that it would be in my
best interest never to watch these appalling injuries as they occur.

Is it any surprise that women generally want to have no part in this man's world?

It has occurred to me that this is a good metaphor for military life in general. You will never truly understand what life in the military is like until you have been "initiated" yourself.

Generally, the initiation for a wife involves no serious injury. Rather, it will be the first time your husband tells you that his leave has been canceled, his pay has been taken away, or he is going on an unscheduled deployment. More personally, it will be the first time you are disrespected by the command, TRICARE refuses to care, or when you need help and no one will assist you.

You will know that you have been fully initiated the first time you realize that everything I have written in this book is entirely true. As offensive as you may find it, I don't make this stuff up. You will be truly initiated and completely capable of dealing with anything when you can look back on everything I have written and laugh hysterically. To joke about the subject matter is to have a truly good attitude and outlook about it, and that is priceless in the military *and* in the world.

CHAPTER 2

Preliminary Concerns

He Actually Did It?

The most overwhelming feeling for most women when their husband or boyfriend enters the military is fear—crushing, constant and eminent fear. It springs from all the uncertainty that a new (unknown) lifestyle offers. The fear of a deployment and being alone. What if something happens to him? If he hurts himself? If he dies? These fears become more solid when reality sets in after he has left. Yes, he actually did it!

I would like to say that none of these bad things will ever happen, but I can't. I also couldn't say it if your husband worked for the Kellogg Corporation. My point is that transfers and accidents happen every day, regardless of career. You must adapt if you wish to be happy.

If your husband has just joined the military and he is currently in training, consider yourself privileged. You are able to go through these changes with your husband, and you have time to adjust. Chances are, you are still in your hometown with your family. Obviously, this is a much more different support system than the military can traditionally offer.

Many a woman is thrown directly into the military lifestyle when she marries an experienced military man. Many times, her respective husband has chosen the military as a career path before the marriage. He has already adapted, leaving her to deal with the confusion by herself.

The only benefit that she can enjoy is the fact that she will not be spending that time away from him while he is in training. It's likely that his next deployment will be the first separation for a couple like this, making the division much more difficult.

It is unproductive and unhealthy to base your entire life around your husband. Having separate lives is critical in any marriage. So don't look at yourselves as a unit never to be parted. Instead, look at yourself as one individual, and your husband as another. You are separate people with separate lives that come together in the middle. Create some things about you and you alone. You will have plenty of time during this initial separation to practice! You will be happier, and your marriage will be stronger for it.

Putting all things aside, I have no doubts that you are searching for knowledge, support and information during this trial separation. This is likely the first time (or the longest time) you have been apart during your entire courtship. You are, no doubt, wondering what he is doing, why he hasn't written, and whether they are treating him okay. You may even be completely freaked out— more so if you have had absolutely no experience with the military and don't know what to expect.

No matter what he is doing, I assure you that he is probably fine. Right now is a time to be concerned with *you*. This chapter is meant to address the concerns you, the brand—spanking-new wife, have during this limbo period in your husband's military career.

What's It Going to Be Like: The 20-Million-Dollar Question

"What's it going to be like?" seems to be the most common question for a newbie to ask. Although this is a typical question, it is often difficult to answer. The military is a different experience for different people and I have no doubts that you will form your own opinions about it over time.

At this point, however, you are probably envisioning every war movie and military drama you have ever seen. Forget all that, as it doesn't apply to you anyway. Life is seldom what is portrayed in the movies. And what it will be like for you is different than what it will be like for him.

So what is left to say? You may develop a new interest in politics because, suddenly, it will affect you directly. You may be overwhelmed with pride for your husband every time you see him in uniform. You will probably find that you have a new attitude about the government and the people in it. You will be on a roller coaster of emotions, for the good times are truly great, while the bad times can be incredibly tragic.

Your house will slowly become filled with green gear and you will become accustomed to military slang. You may have trouble communicating with old friends (civilians) and eventually grow apart from most. You may swear more and complain less.

You will roll your eyes at ordinary marriage problems while dealing with an unaccompanied tour. Your marriage will either be renewed through the joy of a homecoming, or broken by the loneliness of separation and the daily stress of military life.

You will make new friends who can understand what you are going through better than the old ones. The camaraderie you feel towards these friends will be a great experience in and of itself. You will eventually be comfortable going to the exchange and getting on the base without him around. You will become proficient at dealing with life (with or without your husband) and you will adapt to situations that you never imagined you could overcome.

Eventually, you won't even notice a man in uniform because they become so common. You will stare at a man with hair longer than the military allows and wonder what he is doing here. You will move into a house and make it a home, although the area may be foreign to your family. Your children will learn how to salute and their dad will be their hero. He will be your hero.

Life will go on and you will adapt, perhaps, without even noticing. You will realize that the military family is underappreciated and the military man overworked. You will find that family time can be interrupted by work at any given moment. You will see places and things that you never dreamed you would see. You will learn to live on a budget, or choose to live in poverty.

When tragedy befalls the country, you will have trouble seeing past your fear that it means war. You will learn, firsthand, what many people will never really understand: that freedom comes at a price. And while other citizens are busy complaining about how military prisoners are treated by America, you will tearfully send your husband off to catch, fight, or guard those prisoners.

Belonging to a military family is a privilege that many Americans never have. If you survive, even though it's hard, you will all be a little smarter and a little stronger. The key to success in the military is not to take it too seriously. I have rarely come across a long-time military family that has not been able to laugh over the many hardships that have befallen them. And the good often overshadows the bad.

What is it going to be like? It's up to you. I can almost guarantee that your husband will enjoy the many friends he will make and the pride he will feel for his service. The military lifestyle can get the better of many families, but most adapt, and you can too.

So I advise that you delve into your new lifestyle with nothing but enthusiasm and consider the "bad things" to be challenges that you will overcome and be stronger for. If you adapt well, you will become totally comfortable. Eventually, you may find yourself facing the civilian world again and wondering, "What's it going to be like?"

Getting Real: How Often Will He Really be Gone?

Many wives believe themselves incapable of living without their respective husbands' constant presence. Therefore, they are generally concerned with this question during the interminable boot camp period. Some women have a sense of impending doom so overwhelming it causes them to become virtually inconsolable and borderline irrational. It is all so silly and counterproductive.

If you feel this lost, take a good look at your fears. Are you afraid of the uncertainty, or of the deployments? Ask yourself if this concern is helping you in any way to deal with the inevitable situation. Odds are that it's not.

If it is the actual deployments that you are afraid of, let me put your mind at ease. Millions of people join the service every day. Most of them come out alive at the end of whatever term they have chosen. And almost all wives come out in one piece. Some men even find deployments enjoyable. Along with some wives, myself included.

If you are overly concerned about his mortality, stop it. He can die just as easily stepping out to the mailbox and getting hit by a truck. I remember seeing a story in the newspaper about a guy who got hit by a meteorite while standing on his driveway. I'm fairly certain that he wasn't worried about that happening at the time. I have always imagined him standing in front of St. Peter, saying, "Hey, jeez, why me?"

Staying out of the military will not prevent his death; September 11 should have proven that.

There is always some sort of war going on somewhere and our government always seems to make it our national business . . . we are the "nosy neighbors" of the world. In spite of the fact we are not often welcomed, we do a bang-up job of making war (our own and others'). So now, get used to it. Your husband will not be spending every moment of his life with you, and that is no tragedy. Odds are the military won't kill him, and it certainly won't kill you.

There is just no certain answer to the "uncertainty" question. The frequency of deployments cannot be predicted. It's the most frustrating of all answers, but it all just depends. His job, location, hair color, and God knows what else are entered into the military's big equation for who stays and who goes.

Mostly, it seems like they take whoever happens to be handy at the time. I know women who have been without their husbands almost continually for years, as well as women who only had to deal with a few short deployments during their husbands' entire 30-year career.

Like most things in the military, it is essentially the luck of the draw. Sometimes, you win and sometimes you don't. While some may win more often than others, everyone will take their turns dealing with deployments. Rest assured, your husband will (almost certainly) be deployed at one time or another.

That being said, let's try to focus on the things that are really important. If you cling to him, you will never have your own life and you will be miserable while he is away. It is not possible to live independently while at the same time being co-dependent. Whining doesn't gain friends, support, or great sympathy—nor does it bring him home any sooner.

Keep yourself prepared for the times he will leave, but don't fear it. I have always found that the things you fear most will find you, so worrying about his leaving will only make his chances of deployment greater. Also, being constantly worried keeps you from enjoying the time you *do* have with him. He will go, he will come back, and life and the military will go on despite your personal agonies.

Remember: You chose this and now you will be dealing with it, like everyone else does. However, it will be easier for both of you to deal with if you don't treat it as a horrible circumstance that has been unfairly inflicted upon you. I have found that thinking positively has canceled more deployments than it has created.

The WORST Thing EVER!

As we have discussed, many new wives are concerned about separations when faced with their husbands' enlistment. They are also devastated to find out that an unaccompanied one-year tour may be a requirement during their husbands' time in service. Console yourself with THIS thought while hubby is in his boot camp separation or in a mere 3-month deployment.

Being confronted with this issue during a boot camp phone call or hearing about its possibility through an acquaintance can be a terrific shock. This prospect seems devastating, given the time his little bride has already been surviving without him. A one-year unaccompanied tour seems immense, impossible and totally unfair. It's completely unthinkable!

Unaccompanied tours are often endured the first year out of boot camp. He will be spending one year overseas if this happens. If it is unaccompanied, you will not be allowed to go with him.

Your husband may not be required to go right away. Naturally, this tour is determined by the military and neither of you have any choice in the matter once they decide. Remember, though, nothing is certain in the military until it is written down. Don't believe rumors about a tour (or any movement for that matter) until you have those orders in your shaking hands, staring at you in the face.

If your husband plans only on doing his four years and then being discharged, it is possible that this tour will be overlooked and he will not have to go at all. If he is thinking of going career military (planning 20-30 years in service), this is not only a possibility, but is largely unavoidable. In some cases, the military will allow you to accompany him overseas, but it usually involves a longer (three-year) tour and may require a re-enlistment on his part.

Most young servicemen do end up going on unaccompanied tours during their four-year stint. Since this is the case, you must be prepared for the possibility that those unfair, unthinkable and hellacious orders will land on your Honey.

Be aware that this opens whole new opportunities for both of you. As he will be spending a year overseas, experiencing other cultures, you must decide what you will do with your year.

As on long deployments, a wife may opt to live at home with her parents during a one-year tour. This provides the company of extended family, as well as the chance to save some money. Others may decide to go to college, start their own home business, or find another way to amuse themselves while alone.

Whatever you decide to do, I recommend that you not be a stay-at-home wife without any hobbies. Your previously happy home will become a tomb for you. Your loneliness and depression may overcome you, creating more problems for your family.

No matter how wonderful your children may be, moms still need adult interaction on a frequent basis. Your husband's phone calls will not supplement this need. Your best option is to stay busy and accomplish something.

It will do you no good to obsess about this unaccompanied tour which you may have heard so many rumors about. If it happens to you, cross that bridge when you come to it. Perhaps by then, it will just be another deployment. This worry even concerns veteran wives from time to time. Don't become so preoccupied with concern about it that you forget to enjoy your husband when you are together.

Unnecessary concern and worry has no place in a happy home. Never *ever* worry about things over which you have no control. This will help your husband's time in the military breeze by without too much drama or complication.

Your life should be happy despite unfavorable circumstances, not miserable because there is a chance that they will occur. As I have stressed before, your life will go on with or without him there.

When in Doubt, File It. Always.

Truth # 2: *The military just loves paperwork.* Half of our taxes *must be* spent on nothing but paper and on guys to write on the paper. I just know it. If you were present for your husband's enlistment, you may have noticed that he signed an unreasonable amount of paperwork.

The Gov should implement a Workers' Compensation program for all those writing cramps and paper cuts but, y'know, that would require more paperwork. And don't expect it to end there.

Any dealing you ever have with the military will be done entirely in writing. Any minute detail, no matter how insignificant, must be documented, or it never happened. In fact, YOU don't even exist without the correct paperwork, and neither does your husband . . . . or your children. I don't expect this will ever change.

If you think that it does not affect you, you are mistaken. You are the woman and you have better handwriting. The paperwork will be your job from now on. I'd brush up on my signature if I were you . . . or lose my beautiful penmanship.

Since the Gov primarily operates using paperwork, losing one paper causes them to become completely helpless. This always hurts *you.*

There are papers and forms for everything. Computers have changed this for the rest of the world, but the military has yet to catch up. For this reason, I suggest that your first order of business as a military wife is to buy a filing cabinet or devise another method of keeping track of the many files you will accrue.

I never understood the importance of paperwork until the Army lost my medical records when I was ten years old. I was informed that I would be getting all my shots again before I could start school that year. I was confronted with a virtual arsenal of sharp needles. The pain lasted a couple of days, but the memory has lasted forever.

Maybe I was traumatized, but the lesson was learned. I understand the incredible importance of paperwork in the military and their unfortunate tendency towards losing it.

My mother learned the same lesson when transferring to her first duty station from Basic Training. During her in-processing, she discovered that she had misplaced one vital paper, which was missing from the stack. Except for the fortunate goodwill of a finance clerk, our family would have been helpless to rent a home or eat for three months.

Everything must be photocopied. *I cannot emphasize this enough!* Start with medical records; the consequences of losing them are dire. Ask for a copy of all of your family members' records and keep them updated. Always have a current shot record for your husband, yourself, and every child you have.

There is nothing more heartbreaking than watching your husband or child endure his painful shots again because the military lost proof of the last ones. There is no reason for your family to be punished in the name of incompetent record keeping. You can have backups for these records at your request, usually free of charge.

Get a copy of any paperwork that directly relates to the military and you. No matter how inconsequential it may seem, ask yourself what would happen if these records were to be destroyed or lost. Keep in mind, the more vital the piece of paper, the more prone the Gov is to losing it. Coincidence? I think not.

Also, keep records of letters you send to creditors, lawyers, and anyone else whom you are conducting official business with. In the military, it is possible for you to be guilty of something because you have no documentation to back up your story. "Guilty until proven innocent" is alive and well in America, despite rumors to the contrary.

Yes, the military will get into your financial and personal business, especially when creditors or lawyers are calling your husband's company office. No one will stand up for your innocence or take your word for it, so your best bet is to protect yourself and your family by keeping meticulous records.

Be sure to keep copies of your lease agreement and receipts from the landlord, saying that you have paid him on time. If this proves too difficult, ask your landlord to write a letter or sum up your payment history in writing before you move out. This will prove very helpful when attempting to rent another house at your new duty station.

Keep phone, water, electric, and cable company literature available for easy reference when there is a problem. If you work, acquire letters of reference from your employers before you move, to add to your resume. This is also a good idea for your husband as well, because the military is full of transient people who seem to disappear without a trace—current duty station unknown.

Other important papers that you cannot afford to lose are school records, birth certificates, social security cards, bank statements and any other official papers. When in doubt, file it. I have never paid the consequences for filing something that I never looked at again, but I have been sorry for throwing things away.

I find it sad that my family's quality of life can lie in a few files, but if tragedy were ever to befall my dear filing cabinet, we would truly be lost. This is of the utmost importance, and the responsibility will most likely fall upon your shoulders.

Your mission, should you choose to accept it, is to keep dated records of every piece of paper that gains access to your home, has your name on it, or is stuck in any drawer within your immediate area! In other words, buy a filing cabinet, **now**. Color coded, if necessary. I guarantee it will be the best $20 you ever spend.

POA: The VIP of All Paperwork

I have no doubts that you will learn everything you ever wanted to know about paperwork (and more) while your husband is in the military. Fortunately, there is only one paper that is absolutely vital to *you* while your husband is in the military. This is the magical document, the Power of Attorney.

Most military wives choose to maintain a current POA (Power of Attorney) for their husbands' entire stint of service. It can be a lifesaver in almost all situations, but mostly those that require you to conduct your husband's business while he is away. The POA is a piece of paper that is notarized and signed by your husband. It basically gives you the power to conduct his business while representing him.

Although these papers have been easily abused in the past by girlfriends or fiancées, I will trust that your intentions as his wife are in his best interests. This paper allows you to make changes to his checking account, savings account, and life insurance. You may sign contracts for him, including lease and purchase agreements, you may sign away his property, and buy property in his name. You are essentially your husband—as long as you present this paper.

I recommend that every wife be in possession of a current POA while separated from her husband, even if it's only for a week or two. You never know when a situation may arise where it may be required. They are easy enough to acquire (for free) by sending your husband to the JAG (Judge Advocate General) office. It is not even necessary for you to be present in order for your husband to get one for you.

If possible, try and get one before he leaves for boot camp as well. He may call you and want you to take care of some business while he is in training. If you are not yet his wife, he may opt to give the POA to his mother or another family member. If this is the case, they should be taking care of all his business for him.

Humorously enough, the only agency I have ever found that had trouble honoring this paper was a military agency. Therefore, have your husband take care of the military business (if possible) before he leaves. Other than that, be confident about your right to conduct his business while he is away, and try not to abuse your newfound power. I'm sure he does not really need that Mercedes Benz that you have been eyeing . . .

Your New Identity

While your husband is away in boot camp, I strongly suggest that you start committing his social security number to memory. Almost every wife I have ever met has it memorized better than her own. The military will identify you using his SSN. It's very annoying if you have to look it up every time you are asked for it, and I can guarantee the question will be asked frequently.

The next thing that is absolutely essential almost immediately is for you to acquire a government-issued military ID card. You can get one at the nearest base after he graduates from boot camp (as long as you are married). Call the base for details. If your husband is planning on taking leave after boot camp (or doing recruiter's assistance), you can take care of it together while he is home. But make no mistake, you will need one if you plan on partaking in any military benefit whatsoever. Also, any children you may have will need one if they are over 10 years of age.

A helpful tip: Make sure that you are the image of perfection when you are going in to get this done. Even though the military seems virtually incapable of taking good pictures, you will be stuck with what you get.

Be sure and call ahead and find out what paperwork they require before they can issue you a card. Some common items have been marriage and birth certificates, enlistment papers or his military ID, and other official documents of this nature. Come prepared and make it easier on everyone! Especially you. And look pretty because you will have that sucker for a long, long time!

Soldiers and Sailors Civil Relief Act

This is of particular interest to anyone who has debts accrued from before their military life began. Enacted to protect men in the military from more debt than a military budget can handle, it allows for negotiation with creditors.

If your husband has credit cards, car payments, a mortgage, or any other outstanding debt from before he entered active duty, he qualifies. This needs to receive your attention right away if you wish his creditors to address these concerns.

It allows him to lower the interest rates on said debts, as well as negotiate lower payments with the creditors. However, the creditors will not automatically apply these lower rates until they have been notified that he now qualifies for them. He may or may not be instructed about this in boot camp.

If he is no longer in boot camp, you can call the base finance office for more information and assistance with these creditors. They can draft a notification letter for you and allow the savings to commence, or you can just call the creditor. Although this may be a hassle, it can sometimes mean the difference between a financial struggle and being able to pay your bills on time.

After you have sent this information to his creditors, call them in order to ensure that it has been received. Better yet, send it as "return receipt requested." Illegal or not, many of these letters have been "lost in the mail," and the man is never the wiser.

It is your responsibility to fight for these rights because they will not be handed to you. Always keep a copy of your notification letter and the dates that they were sent (or send them via certified mail) so that there can be no argument about receipt.

Keep in mind that this will only protect your husband from things over which he has no control, such as being sued while on deployment, or debts from before the military service began. It will give you no relief for debts that you have since acquired. If you would like more information about the SSRA, call the JAG office or talk to your sponsor. If your husband is still in boot camp, his recruiter can often be helpful on matters such as these.

Letters to Hell (I Mean . . . Basic Training!)

If you are like most women, the time preceding boot camp and your husband's enlistment went rather quickly. As soon as he gets on that airplane, however, the clock stops ticking and it seems like he will be gone for an eternity.

This is often a great hardship to survive because phone calls and communications are severed during this time. Get used to it. This is your first bitter taste of the worst that the military has to offer—and it's not pleasant for your husband either. You can find strength in the fact that after boot camp, usually, you will have more contact with him. You can also comfort yourself by remaining massively distracted. Chocolate's good.

The main concern that you have to focus on is writing him encouraging letters. You will probably receive no mail from him at first. After the initial in-processing, the letters become more frequent and you will have something to look forward to on a weekly basis. Even if your husband is not a writer, he will be in boot camp. My husband never wrote a word before boot camp, and hasn't since then. But while he was there, he churned out letters like they were going out of style!

I have heard many complaints regarding the lack of speed with which mail is delivered to him. Some wives opt to send letters via priority mail and spend tons of money to ensure that their husbands get the letters sooner. Despite these efforts, priority mail often gets lost in the sea of mail that boot camps receive on a daily basis. Also, just because the mail has been received does not mean that it will be distributed immediately.

Keep in mind that your husband's contact with you is not the military's prime concern at this time—or any time, for that matter. They don't care. Also, know that almost every man in boot camp has an SO at home who is employing the same mailing strategy as you.

In boot camp, letters from home are often treated as a privilege and can be withheld if the drill instructor feels the urge. However, to my knowledge, the military has no time to be pre-screening your letters for content. I doubt that they have the time or manpower for such an exhaustive endeavor.

It is, however, *your* job to screen letters for content, and it is wise to keep your contact with him relatively positive and upbeat. He is helpless to remedy the problems going on at home. Telling him how horrible things are will only make him feel bad and may impair his progress. If his progress is hindered, he will only remain in boot camp longer . . . and no one wants that.

Under no circumstances is it wise of you to send him anything that you (or he) would not want to be viewed by others. Maybe many others. Drill instructors live by embarrassing these men based on things found in letters from home. To illustrate my point, let me regale you with a tale of woe from "wives' boot camp."

I met a girl who sent a pair of her favorite underwear to her fiancé in boot camp. Upon receiving his package, he was able to open it in front of everyone in his barracks. When the contents of the package were revealed, the DI just smiled. He then confiscated them and sent everyone to bed.

The next morning, as the snickering recruits filed past the company office, her stringy pink panties hung in public view under a sign that read "motivation." The panties remained there until the graduation.

The girl was unaware that her underwear had been used to motivate countless recruits until after the graduation ceremony, when the DI came to greet her. In his hand, he held her unmentionables. He presented them to her with no shame and said, "Ma'am, I just wanted to let you know that these have inspired many men."

If this is a scene that you would rather avoid, try not to make the same mistake. And no naked pictures either!

Boot Camp Is Over; Kiss Him Goodbye Again.

AIT, MCT, AFT, LMNOP—no matter what they call it, you (and he) will be enduring it. Your husband's schooling. At last, boot camp is over and that wonderful 10 days of leave has come and gone. You are saying goodbye once again and it's still hard.

Generally, this period is less strict and you will be allowed more contact with him. He may also be getting days off once in a while. But they will seldom be off "for sure" because if one man messes up, they will all be punished. This is the military way.

At this time, you have probably got a general idea about the military. You may already know what duty station he will be assigned to and you will certainly have noticed the changes in him when visiting after basic training. You are most likely still filled with that nagging uncertainty about what the future holds.

What is your husband's job? It is really not relevant. No matter what his individual job may be, he is now a part of a whole working family functioning to protect our country. Every job in the military is considered important.

Now, the challenge of his schooling has arrived, and it is time to confront it. Many wives feel the need to set up camp wherever her husband may be schooling. This is not a good idea. Chances are, this preliminary training will last only a couple months before he is sent elsewhere for job training. They are also still withholding his housing allowance because he will reside in quarters. In other words, if you join him for training, you will be bearing the cost, and you can't afford it.

I have seen many women do this and it usually creates more problems. The demands of school are many and your hours together are few. Are you going to be able to deal with being so close to him and yet never have the pleasure of his company? Are you willing to endure the loneliness and financial hardship that it requires in exchange for only a few rewards? Not likely. Chances are, you are better off staying put until he completes preliminary schooling.

In my experience, underlying fears are responsible for this urge to join him. Do you really feel that you need to baby-sit your husband? Since the military is no longer "policing" his free time, maybe all hell will break loose. He'll likely go nuts.

The ability to trust your husband is crucial in the military. I find that fear, more than anything, drives women to give up so much to join their husbands at school. Maybe, he will go out drinking with the guys! So what? He can do that while you are there, too. You won't stop him if that's what he wants to do. So while your fears may have a real basis for whatever reason, the idea that you can prevent him from drinking (or whatever it is you are concerned about) is an illusion. Trust your husband and save your money.

Allow him this time to bond and make friends. Camaraderie is crucial for the military to work effectively. You want your husband to be making friends because someday, the same people might rescue him from danger or even save his life.

There is a good chance these buddies of his will become useful to you in the future as well. I cannot tell you how many times one of my husband's buddies took on the role of baby-sitter, duty taker, or money lender while we had more pressing business to attend to.

Allow the military to work its magic. All this perpetual male bonding would probably sicken even the strongest of women, but it is all worth it in the long run.

In the end, when you consider all the military benefits, the thing that you will remember most are the wonderful people who have touched your life. Camaraderie and friendship in tough times is the greatest benefit the military ever had. As they say, "Misery loves company," and the military is very good at providing misery.

If he is going to language school or somewhere that will take a considerable amount of time, it is much more economical to move to where he is schooling. However, in *most* cases, schooling lasts less than six months and it's just not worth it. If you must, save your money for a trip halfway through the 6-month period. Better yet, just save it for the deposit on your home at his *permanent* duty station.

The truth is that this limbo period is nothing compared to the rest of his career. It is only the beginning of his career. Consider his boot camp and job school as *training for you* while you still have the support of your hometown family and friends to make it through. You won't have that in the "real military."

It is unlikely that when he is sent to the "real military," things will be as easy as you may imagine. It is certain that you will not be able to stay with him or even visit him while he is on that inevitable 6-month deployment overseas.

You are undermining the practice you need by living with him at school. It is a lot easier to let go while he is perfectly safe in Mississippi training, than it is to let go while he is overseas at the war. This training is not only crucial for him, it is critical for *you*.

The Stuff That Benefits Are Made Of

There are women who seek military men for the benefits alone. I have also heard rumors about so-called contract marriages. The man will marry the woman so he can have extra money and the woman will have the benefits. I don't know how often these things happen, or even if they do. What it does show me, however, is that the benefits the military provides for its service members and families are highly desirable.

Even if you are not engaging in a "contract marriage," your benefits will be helpful to you. I have met many women who get upset over stereotypes about this kind of thing. Their friends will wonder why they would marry a man who is gone all the time. It obviously cannot be for love—therefore, it must be for the money. Anyone who has been in the military for a single pay period knows that this is completely untrue. Contract marriages are for benefits, always, always, always. And the benefits often leave much to be desired, especially with such a puny paycheck.

One very big concern of most women who are new to this is "When do the benefits start?" The answer is, when you are married . . . period. If you are currently married and he is in boot camp, you will have to wait at least until he graduates before you can acquire a military ID. Your military ID is the key to all benefits (along with his social security number, of course).

If you are not yet married and you are pregnant with his child, TRICARE will not pay for your pre-natal care. They will cover the child once it is born. If you are in this situation, I recommend either marrying or getting on Medicaid. There are *no* benefits without an ID card.

The military will also not allow you to reside in base housing with him if you are not married. You are more than free to attempt living in town together, but if he has no dependents and is enlisted, he may be required to live in the barracks. This means that you will receive no BAH (Basic Allowance for Housing). It is mighty difficult to live on basic military salary alone.

If you are married, these benefits may be difficult to appreciate, given the amount of work your husband seems to be doing. Try and remember that there are many women in this world who would give anything to have these benefits for herself and her family. There are people struggling to have what is so easily taken for granted by us, military wives. You will learn about this when he finally separates from the military.

Appreciating these little things will keep you happy. Try not to think about your ghetto-like base house and that mistake the doctor made last time. In other words, focus on the positive. You and your husband are together (most of the time) and that is all you wanted when you married him, right?

Who Is Obligated to Whom?

If you are one of the lucky ones who has been promised an enlistment bonus, I hope you have got it on paper! There are many ways for the military to pay this back to you.

A lot of times, you will get a small part of the bonus up front and are paid the rest little by little, in each paycheck. This, to me, seems like the best way because you will be making a little more each month than everyone else. This gives you a financial headstart.

If your husband has been in for a while and you have yet to see the bonus, check out the LES (Leave and Earning Statement). It's possible that you didn't even notice it. Hard to believe that you are actually getting paid more than everyone else is, huh? Don't worry, that is completely normal. No one gets paid what they are actually worth. Look at me, I'm worth millions, but for some reason, my husband's LES does not reflect that value.

If you are like almost everyone else, you were under the impression that you will be getting paid a lot in the military. It was this big money-making opportunity, right? Damn those recruiters! This is as far from reality as you can get. (Refer to truth #3 in Chapter 3.) You will also not be getting paid horribly as long as you are able to live within your means. The military is all about the benefits, but the money ain't one of them, let me tell you.

Most women are comfortable while their husbands are in the military. New wives soon come to realize that the paychecks are steady and the medical care is semi-free. The thing that some don't understand is quite a vital piece of knowledge. There is no "free lunch," even in the military.

You have a contract with the government and you are obligated to them. They are not, and I repeat, they are not in any way, shape, or form obligated to you or to your husband. They do not owe you anything. They can kick him out at any given moment if they feel like it.

While his getting kicked out may sound like a blessing to you now, you will be mighty upset if your husband goes through 2 months of boot camp only to be held back for 6 months while he sits on a board, getting kicked out because he fractured a nose hair.

The military is not required to pay you. They will do what they want when they get around to it. In general, your money will be on time, so don't let me scare you too badly. All I am saying is that if Sergeant Major Annoyance accidentally trips over your husband and decides that it's your husband's fault, he can do whatever he wants in order to punish him for this offense. Why? The military owns him, that's why. They do follow rules, but these rules are made up by the military to protect the military and are almost never in the best interest of your husband.

As far as kicking him out of the military is concerned, this mostly happens during boot camp. And since he is obligated to the military and the military has no obligation to him, they will probably not pay him. In fact, they may even let him sit around for months in boot camp, doing nothing while they take their sweet time doing (you guessed it) discharge *paperwork*.

The military scrutinizes every cent that they give out. A medical board convenes precisely for this reason. To decide what his injury is worth in dollars. There are also quite a few other reasons to kick your husband out other than just medical. So many that I will not go over them here. Read the UCMJ (Uniform Code of Military Justice) for more information about why they might kick him out or even send him to military prison.

All you really need to know is that if the military decides to screw you, they will do so. They have no morals or sense of humor that I am aware of. They are not required to have them, and I doubt that they want them. Accept this and keep it in the back of your mind. Don't be surprised if they do decide to kick him out with nothing someday. It *is* tremendously unfair. Life is not fair, sweetie, and the military continues to prove it.

Of Slimeballs and Shitheads

No matter what your opinion is about your husband's recruiter, he can be a great asset to you while your husband is in basic training and preliminary schooling. He is a wealthy source of information that you can generally take advantage of at your leisure.

The recruiter can answer any specific questions you may have (that this book may not answer for you) during this time. It is his job to follow through on the enlistment. He has made the sale and you are responsible for making sure he follows through with the support you deserve.

Many people have a negative attitude about recruiters. They find it appalling that the recruiter lied to them. This is generally an accepted part of military life. However, I think it is fair to say that no one (except, perhaps, another recruiter) can quite understand the job and stresses a recruiter must deal with. These men work 16-hour days and are constantly trying to reach a quota. If your husband is ever flagged for recruiting duty, you may understand the complications involved with this job.

That being said, "Let the buyer beware." And since your husband has already enlisted, there is nothing to be done about it now aside from learning everything you can. Note that I never say that these slimy, lying recruiters are not going straight to hell. But they can be useful.

Utilize these men to your advantage and treat them as a friend. Even if you hate everything about the military, I guarantee you will still learn something from your military experience. In this way, the recruiter has done you and your husband a favor.

I find that most recruiters do not lie outright, but they are often misheard because what an applicant *wants* to hear is far different from what the recruiter is actually saying. Many young people make mistakes like this. Also, many recruiters are guilty of playing up the good things and not mentioning the bad things, unless specifically asked. That's the job!

After your husband is safely shipped off to boot camp, this man has no reason to mislead you. He has made his quota and he is moving on. If you crave knowledge or have questions, do not hesitate to call him. Your husband is not the only one making a sacrifice here. Often, the recruiter is your first and only contact with your husband and his new military life. Use him and abuse him, baby! Make him earn his money!

I Hate the Military!

Me too. Who doesn't? Everyone goes through a "disenchantment phase." Sometimes. it will last for a month or so, other times, it will last for the entire 4 years. What can you do about it? Nothing, really.

I believe that the military should have some kind of 1-800 number to call when you just really need to yell at them. Like when your husband does not arrive home on the third "scheduled arrival home date." Unfortunately, the military is not this customer friendly. I guess it's time to get used to that. But keep in mind that not even customer-oriented organizations are very customer friendly when you are complaining. At least, the military is honest about not caring.

So you must find other ways of taking out your frustration. Many wives resort to smoking or drinking, and bitching at their husband about it. But I have heard of some much more creative ways of dealing with this "I hate the military!" phase.

I once met a girl who iron-transferred a picture of Bin Laden on a pillow while her husband was in Afghanistan. She literally beat this pillow daily until she felt better. I personally enjoy going to the shooting range. Listening to nasty, loud, and angry music in the car never hurt anyone, either.

Of course, there are much more effective ways suitable for women with children, or for those of you who are more "laid back." Hobbies are a good creative outlet. You will find that scrapbooking is very popular and rewarding for many women. There are several Internet wives' clubs where you can vent to sympathizers like yourself. Also, there are a great many women conducting profitable and rewarding home businesses, like Mary-Kay or Princess House Crystal. And there is always a wonderful market in military towns for out-of-home day cares.

Any way you choose to vent your frustrations and soothe your soul is good. This means many things to many people. I cannot stress enough that you do need a hobby, or at least, a job. I have chosen to write this book in addition to a number of other part-time endeavors. Build a life that you are happy with and can be proud of. This way, when your husband comes home, you will have something to talk about as well aside from him. That way, you don't have to constantly listen to those boring, old war stories.

Good Things

I realize that I have made many negative comments relating to the military, and I will probably make many more. But if you are feeling overwhelmed and need some encouragement, read this. This is the big "catch" of the military. This is why everyone is here and people will continue to be drawn to the military, despite the consequences. These are the great things about the military that every civilian family searches for.

Many civilians don't fully understand these perks and even say that we are undeserving at times. This is completely untrue. Anything the military gives to you is deserved. You deserve it for putting up with them! Ask your husband if the military has ever given him anything that he has not earned. Don't listen to anything any civilian ever tells you about your benefits unless he works at the finance office.

Every military wife I have ever known has had some deep concerns regarding her husband's discharge. Like many wives, they came into the military not knowing what it was all about . . . sometimes, right out of high school. Then, faced with the possibility of getting out, they feel their entire support system collapse under them. Here are the major things that they took for granted and now miss. Here are the things that I think about when I am completely fed up with the military and everything it stands for . . .

1. *Paid leave.* Your husband's pay will never change because he took leave. He will get paid the same for 2 weeks of leave that he would if he was to work 2 weeks. Comparable to civilian jobs, this is almost unheard of, especially when you throw into the mix that he gets about 30 days of leave per year.

2. *Full medical and dental.* Any ailment that may be of concern to you is completely covered by TRICARE. Sure, there are some exceptions, but anything major and necessary will be covered for yourself and for your children. You will never have to worry about medical bills or expenses (for the most part) as long as you are in the military.

3. *Life Insurance.* The military covers your husband as long as he does not refuse it. This policy does not exclude acts of war, so you will be taken care of if there is any kind of unfortunate accident.

4. *Leniency towards family problems.* I know this sounds contradictory, but my husband has gotten off work many times to take care of important business that cannot be taken care of on weekends. This includes going to the DMV or Social Security office, as well as doctor's visits when I was pregnant. As long as there is a valid reason for him to leave, they will usually let him. And they will not dock his pay for it.

5. *Job security.* There is just no way in hell he is going to be fired from the military. Trust me. If he has an injury, it will take them *months* to get rid of him. You will not end up

unable to pay your rent and buy diapers because his employer laid him off.

6. *Respect.* This is kind of an iffy one. There are some who respect the military and others who don't. Either way, you will have pride when you tell people your husband is in the military, and your husband will have more respect for himself.

7. *No college required.* Many enlisted men join right out of high school. I don't think that he could accomplish as good a livelihood with a civilian job and no education. As bad as it is, he can advance. It is just not comparable to flipping burgers.

8. *Support.* No matter where you look on a military base, you will find a support group of military wives. Even if you don't, you will have a base full of bored women who will be thrilled to have a friend like you.

9. *Credit.* This is a topic near and dear to my heart. You also have to be careful with this one. Many businesses will give you instant credit if you are military. This can help you, and it could hurt you as well. Credit is a good thing if used wisely. Be cautious with these pre-approval deals and don't allow yourself to be overwhelmed financially. The military has your back on this one.

    These businesses feel comfortable approving you because they know if you default on a loan, the military will take it from your check and give it to them without asking what you think about it. You must also be cautious about instant credit because the finance rates are often outrageous. A loan shark is often open handed, but the interest rates are killer. This is why you must be cautious.

10. *Free college.* This one does not apply to you. But it is comforting to think that when and if your husband decides

to go to college, you will not be dealing with that financial burden. And if you look hard enough, you can find military spouses' benefits as far as college goes. You just have to know where to look.

So I'm Not Helping?

You can look anywhere you need to for inspiration in the military. Be it the Bible, this book, or a Tony Robbins cassette. Different things work for different people and it will always be so.

I choose to turn to friends during times of hardship and laugh at my situation. You may choose a different method, but I would like to suggest that it not be negativity. Don't make yourself and others miserable. You are very privileged to be a part of an organization that can leave you a cultured and wise individual, even if it *does* feel like abuse in the process (no doubt, it will for a while).

Maybe, you already have completed the basic training and schooling processes, or will soon—this is only the tip of the iceberg. You have already experienced boot camp separation. It is now time to experience the real thing. Base housing, new stations, moving, the exchange, and all the other wonderful things that come along with the military. While the preceding process has been a challenge, your greatest challenges are yet to come.

Plenty of support systems and methods are in place for military wives and families. The challenge is to find one that works for you. If you decide that clubs don't work, try the Internet, self-help books, or friends. This being said, not everyone chooses support that is specifically tailored to the military—and there are no rules on how far you can go.

Many find support for themselves through Weight Watchers, Bingo, work, and even college. There are also those rare leaders who have started their own businesses, sponsored their own clubs, and improved their bases for those who would follow them.

Always remember that no one wants to be around a whiner, and that bored people are boring. You can make things better for yourself and those around you if you are conscious of your actions and words. Perhaps, if you have trouble adjusting, it's because of your attitude. The most important thing to do if you are unable to find help is to take your own initiative. *You can find support almost anywhere, but it will hardly ever find you.*

Q & A

Q. So what *can* I count on from the military?

A. Nothing.

Q. I think when a guy signs up for the military, there should be a mandatory meeting at the nearest base that all SOs have to attend. They should tell us what to expect, how to deal with things, etc . . .

A. They do have classes like that, but you have to find them. The government cannot require a civilian to do anything except pay taxes . . . and isn't that enough?

Q. I was wondering how many duty stations you usually get, or do you just stay at one base your entire 4 years?

A. He is the military's puppet; they can do what they want. Depending on his job and the military's mood, you could do either.

Q. I am such a planner, it is driving me crazy not to know things!

A. Get used to it.

Q. How do you handle that someone else chooses where you will go and when that will happen?

A. I *do* choose where I go and when it will happen. The military just likes to correct me when I am wrong.

Q. Can I meet new people while my husband is in the military?

A. Um, yes. You will meet an infinite number of people. Some you will like, some you will hate, and some you won't care about one way or the other. Remember that the same applies to you.

Q. The military is so slow and sometimes unconcerned with our lives!!!

A. What exactly do you mean by *sometimes*?

Foreword: For the Fiancée

Planning a wedding is usually a huge part of getting married. Many women who are currently "married to the military" (myself included) have opted for the traditional military wedding. No, not a man in his uniform and a woman in her wedding dress. Rather, a man and woman in front of the nearest Justice of the Peace at the local courthouse of whatever godforsaken base they happen to be stationed in. If you are choosing the nontraditional wedding, with all the relatives and a dress and all the unnecessary stuff, there is one thing you need to know above all else: Do not put a date on anything! This includes the invitations, if possible. Definitely not on the napkins, favors, cutting tools, nothing!

I once met a girl who was inducted into the Marine Corps' way of life early through this innocent mistake. She got her military welcome long before that slap on the butt with the sword! After planning her wedding for nearly a year, she had the date set in stone. When the Marines kept her husband past her date, everything was ruined. I'm certain that it was no less than a complete disaster.

They were forced to postpone, and her budget did not allow for her to purchase new dated materials. So she kept the old dates on everything in the wedding. She still has those cake cutters with the wrong date on them. I am sure that she is constantly reminded by these mementos to never to write a date in stone again. That is, at least until her husband has his discharge papers in hand. She thanked the military for giving her the first taste of being a military wife so early. I am sure that she's had many lessons from them since.

Many women tell me that if they had known what being a military wife entailed, they would never have committed. I disagree, and I think you will too. The military is just not worth getting that upset over. As a fiancée, I bet you are confident that you can handle anything as long as the two of you can be together. Keep that attitude for the next few years and I am sure you will succeed.

CHAPTER 3

"All You Can Be," for the Little Woman

Section 1: The Difference

A wife has several responsibilities, including my least favorite: childbearing. A military wife has to deal with it almost twice as much. You will be going above and beyond the call of duty frequently. The Service presents challenges for wives which are not only unique, but which require more work. It's a bum deal, let me tell you. Your husband's career will frequently render him unable to perform activities that you may already be accustomed to him doing. There are a many things you must be capable of by yourself.

I perform quite a few tasks, in addition to my traditional "wifely duties" and in the middle of it all, I still somehow find time for myself. Most often, I find that the areas of expertise covered in the following chapter are characteristics of the most successful military wives I have encountered.

In the real world, these chores are generally split, shared, or even taken care of by the hubby himself. Not anymore, Superwife! Get busy learning the following if you are not completely proficient already. It also couldn't hurt to learn how to change a tire and an air filter. While it often seems unfair that the weight of the household seems to fall on your shoulders, over time, you might become a complete control freak. In the future, your husband's taking over may result in complete disaster.

Be thankful that it is you in control. Always know that the house runs smoothly because of you. You just allow your husband to believe that he wears the proverbial pants in the family. He will know the truth when you leave him for a few days to visit your parents and everything starts falling down around him. Resulting in . . . that's right, disaster.

Brilliant Accountant

Truth # 3: *You will not be making good money.* What I mean by this is that not only will you not make "good" money, you will make almost *no* money. Learn to spin straw into gold immediately. If you find this task daunting, then you may want to consider budgeting. Cut out anything and everything that gives you pleasure.

Once this is done, you will find that (while you continue to breathe and eat) you are completely void of entertainment. Get used to it. Maybe when your husband gets promoted, you can finally hook up for that fancy cable TV you have been hearing so much about. It is essential to the livelihood of yourself and your family that you manage money like an expert. Not just an expert, but a pro. Not only will you be making no money, but you will also have many expenses.

I have noticed that every time my finances are under control, something always comes up. If it is usually your husband's responsibility to pay the bills . . . well, have you seen him around lately? The point is that he will not always be around to pay the electric bill, so hopefully, you can take care of it proficiently.

Keep in mind that your goal is to acquire as few expenses as possible. I myself have a husband who likes to have the biggest and the best of everything. You will have to be the bad guy at times and tell the salesman "no" while your husband cowers.

My husband picked up the phone one day only to receive a recording—one of those telemarketer holds. While he sat there saying nothing, I asked why he was not talking. He related to me that he was "holding for an important message." These men are strong, but it seems that they can stand up to anyone, except a salesman. Must be another one of those big military secrets that they don't want the bad guys to know, lest we lose all future wars to salesmen.

Before I learned about budgeting, our expenses raged out of control and we sometimes had no money to buy food. Our phone was shut off several times and so was our electricity. Although we were living in utter poverty and struggling to save for food, the military maintained that we weren't being underpaid, we were just overspending.

After examining our monthly expenses carefully, the military finance professional concluded that we needed to pay off our debts. No doubt, you can believe, this helped us immensely. We sat in silence during the car ride home, realizing we were doomed to deal with this problem alone.

Mostly, you will have no money to manage. You will have enough to pay the basic bills and buy groceries. You will not be living in the lap of luxury. The time when you need to be an expert is when an unexpected expense comes up and you have to cut corners in your bill paying to scrape together enough cash for this nuisance.

It will help to keep a savings account, although you will rarely have extra money to put into it. When you get some extra money, you would probably prefer to spend it on something that gives you pleasure—WARNING: Don't do it!

The military lifestyle holds many hidden costs and these "unexpected" expenses present themselves every month. You may think (for example) that his uniforms are paid for, but you are mistaken! A set of good BDUs (Battle Dress Uniform, also known as cammies) can cost $40-60, and the prices are going up with the introduction of the new, more "stylish" ones.

You must also consider the price of alterations. Every time your husband is promoted or grows thinner or fatter, all of his uniforms must be upgraded. Uniforms other than BDUs can cost in excess of $400. The military does give a clothing allowance. On average, this clothing allowance is $100-200 per year. Make sure and use it wisely! I have trouble believing that Yoda could manage on that budget.

The importance of budgeting can be summed up with this little economic study conducted by me . . . My best friend and her husband lived in the same town as we did. Her husband held the same rank as mine. Also, we were the same age, made the same amount of money, and had the same number of children.

Her family chose to live without furniture while they saved to buy the less expensive kind, for cash. We financed our furniture for 2 years and bought the most expensive stuff. They drove a used car that was given to them by their parents, while we paid on a $30,000 truck loan. They never spent more on their credit cards than they could afford to pay off, while we paid the minimum balances on our maxed-out cards.

While she and her husband were enjoying their lives together (going out to movies and dinner), my husband and I sat in our house with our truck and useless, expensive furniture. We spent our lives crunching numbers and wishing we had more money. Eventually, we learned, but it cost us a lot of hard work and sacrifice (not to mention time and money) to get back out of the hole. We lost at least a year of happiness together for that stupid truck and some expensive furniture, which worked just the same as my friend's furniture and vehicle.

She knew how to be an expert accountant. She understood many things which have taken me years to learn and which I continue to struggle with. I have no doubt you will learn these lessons. You can learn it from me, or you can learn it from reality. Your choice! The military will never be able to bail its servicemen out of financial challenges. That's why they have wives, I guess. The following are some tips that I have used myself, successfully.

Ways to cut corners in your budget

- Clip coupons, even if you are going to the commissary.
- Turn off your cable/internet, or just cut it down to basic. (Try not to spend the excess cash at the video store.)
- Do not pay for anything they have on base, including your husband's gym membership.
- Do not get your hair or nails done professionally, unless it is for a special occasion.

- Go out to eat only once a month . . . or less.
- Don't buy junk food, only the necessities. Make a grocery list before you go shopping and stick to it.
- Do not go to the mall or other stores where you will be tempted to buy things that you "need."
- Do not make any compulsive purchases. This includes door-to-door salesmen or 1-800 number orders and the ever-popular "window shopping." This rule includes your husband and his impulses.
- Turn off the long-distance service on your phone. Only use a phone card with a reasonable rate. Try www.bigzoo.com.
- Do not acquire any credit card unless you are certain that you can and will use them responsibly.
- If you need a loan, go to a military organization, such as Navy or Army Relief. They will give it to you interest free. This saves you a lot of money.
- Call around about your auto insurance and see if switching companies will get you a lower rate.
- Quit smoking or cut down. If this proves impossible, switch to a cheaper brand. The same goes for alcohol. They are both expensive habits.
- Gratefully accept hand-me-downs or shop at the Goodwill, especially for children's clothing and toys.
- Acquire renter's insurance. You will pay a small monthly fee, but if something from your home is damaged/stolen/destroyed, it will pay for itself the first time you use it.
- If your husband takes care of the finances, make sure he consults with you about it. Discuss ways to cut the budget with him if you are struggling. It will be your responsibility the first time he gets deployed.
- Read finance books. Use the worksheets they provide if you think they may be helpful.
- Consider getting a job if you are hurting for money. If kids complicate things, consider starting a home day care or other work-from-home opportunity. There is also much money to be made in a military town, working as a bartender or waitress.

- If you wish to purchase a big-ticket item, such as a computer or television, save your money until you can buy it for cash. It will save you a lot of money in finance charges. In military towns, finance charges tend to be higher, so if you must finance, it would benefit you to go outside town for better rates.
- Happily utilize programs like WIC and food stamps if you qualify. If the government is not paying you enough, you should not feel bad about asking for more.
- Place your credit cards in a container filled with water. Once frozen it will take at least an hour to dry. This helps control impulse buys.
- Carpool to save on gas.
- Check base newspapers for free activities in your area.
- Ask for military discounts. A lot of theme parks, theatres and sporting events offer them.
- Pack your own food when going on outings. Have your husband eat a sack lunch at work rather than buying it.
- Buy memberships or year passes to places that you often visit.
- If you are an avid reader, find and use the local library.
- Buy generic.
- Buy CD's, tapes and video games used.
- Don not accrue late fees, pay on time.
- When renting movies, return them on time to avoid late fees.

Use your common sense. Always look before you leap. Try not to finance anything. If you must finance, make sure the interest rate is reasonable and you can afford the payments in your payment plan.

It does not take a rocket scientist to conclude that a manicure and pricey vehicles are not necessities. Consider carefully whether you are acting from *need* or want. Never commit to something you are feeling uncomfortable about and follow your instincts. Ask yourself if the purchase is necessary. And if it is, can you find a cheaper one?

Hail, the Computer Guru!

One skill that I highly recommend that any military wife acquire is computer ability. You will almost certainly be living far from family and friends. The computer will not only help you to communicate conveniently, but it will also allow you to view job ads or rental homes in places that are far away. This comes in handy at moving time.

Your family will miss you and want to hear from you frequently. If you have children, your responsibility to keep the grandparents and other family "in the loop" is even greater. Sending e-mails and instant messaging will save you hundreds of dollars in phone bills. Since e-mail is sometimes easier than a phone to access while your husband is on deployment, you may also have more contact with him.

If your family craves more than the occasional e-mail, you may want to consider starting a web page on which to post photos and updates on, particularly if you have a very large extended family. I find that my web page enables me to share more pictures with interested parties while saving me money on postage and photo production.

Consider also the conveniences of Internet banking. You can also download on-line coupons for shopping at your local PX and exchange. Phone cards are particularly cheap when acquired on the Internet and there are also tons of websites about saving money, being married, safety, cooking recipes, etc. If you wish to communicate with others like yourself, you can join e-mail groups which will put you in contact with other women around the world. I conduct most business on-line in my home. Much like my filing cabinet, I would be lost without my computer. I seldom make phone calls or go out to purchase something that is readily available to me via computer.

If you are not yet familiar with the computer, get on-line and explore. You will soon realize the advantages the computer can offer you. You can also take classes at the local college on web publishing, or read tutorials on-line.

The advantages of the Internet are at your fingertips. It's all about how you use it. If you don't own a computer, see if you can acquire a hand-me-down from a friend or relative. You can also consider buying a refurbished computer, or pick up a used one in the local paper. Used computers are often cheaper and often do the job just as well. If you decide to buy a new computer, I suggest you not finance it, for the reasons we have already discussed. Either way, computer talent always looks good on a resumé and is useful in many diverse jobs. If you are not yet computer savvy, it is good to learn, even if you think you will never use it.

I Want YOU . . . to Be My Secretary!

"Honey, put this in a safe place so I don't lose it."

"Babe, please call the hospital and tell them I'll miss my appointment."

"Did anyone call for me?"

Yes, soon it will hit you. You are his secretary. Among your many responsibilities and talents, secretarial skills are important. They are even more essential with the excess paperwork and hassle that the military creates. But military or not—you will always be his secretary in one way or the other.

You are responsible for any and all papers that come in and out of your home. Even if you have never seen the document in question, when it's lost, you will be blamed. Like Roseanne Barr says, the family believes that a uterus is a tracking device.

For this reason, it is important to run all papers by him before throwing them away. This includes scraps in the pockets of his uniform and the crumpled messes that he throws under the bed.

Even a nameless phone number chicken-scratched on a napkin may be needed for further reference. Even if he says "Toss it," you may still want to keep it in a temp file for a while. I have already discussed the importance of a filing cabinet. What I may have failed to mention is that *you* will be maintaining the files within it. Annoying or not, you *do* want it this way. If your husband starts filing things incorrectly, you will not find anything, ever. And you will *still* be responsible.

Often I find important documents "filed" in a drawer or sometimes, even under the seat of his car. Anything that he checks out of your filing cabinet must be returned to you—and you need to tell him this. Otherwise, the next time he wants it, he will accuse you of losing it and figuratively, burn you at the stake . . . until he finds it in the back of the car, that is. Then he might feel bad.

You will also be learning the importance of phone skills. Man, those secretaries have got it hard. You will call everyone from the electric company, to the command, to the hospital. I have even been requested to make his personal calls . . . to his friends! "Get PFC Johnson on the line, will you?" Yep.

The upside: Mail duty is all yours. You may find yourself sorting through the bills and creating a system to organize it. It may take a while to find a system that works for you. Suggestion: Do not, under any circumstances, allow him to get to the mailbox before you! Those important bills will be late because he'll file them in the back of the car or under the seat. Sigh.

We *Still* Have to Pay TAXES?

Yes, I know. It sucks. Being the secretary and record keeper, this automatically leaves you with the dreaded bills. But you must also consider taxes, even more dreaded than the bills. I have found this to be one of my greatest challenges.

Naturally, you can pay someone else to do your taxes. You can also go to the finance office on base and have it done for free. I have problems with this because those people will not be held accountable if they make a mistake. There are no guarantees.

I once knew a couple who got a huge refund after the finance office (for the military) did their taxes. A few months later, an error was discovered and they were forced to cough up the balance of several hundred dollars.

I believe you should do your own taxes at least once. Most tax institutions will charge you as much as $200 for an instant refund, while the IRS generally only takes a couple of weeks to send a check. I think $200 is worth the wait. You can use one of a number of on-line services and e-file for about $6.

At least, if you do it yourself, no one can come back later and punish you for someone else's mistake. Only for your own!

Your husband must also pay state taxes in his home state, that is, his "home of record" state—where he first joined the military. If you are lucky enough to come from a state that does not require taxes, then you are home free.

However, you (the wife) are considered resident of whatever state you are living in (unless you are also under active duty). If you get a civilian job, you will be required to pay state taxes in the state where you live. The same applies if your husband gets a civilian job in addition to his military duties.

To obtain state tax forms from his home of record, you can go to www.irs.gov on-line, or call your home state tax office. You can obtain a federal and current state tax form and booklet at the local post office. Hint: Grab a couple of everything, in case you mess up! Always keep copies of tax records. They are paperwork, after all.

If you are claiming deductions for things such as uniform costs, you must have all receipts on file. Keep a copy of your original W2 and W4 forms. If you choose to pay someone else to do your taxes, make sure you double-check everything before you allow them to file it. Make certain to understand what your preparer did. Remember, *you* take the hit for any errors. Have them explain to you why you do or do not qualify for certain deductions. You can never be too careful when dealing with the Gov.

Not a Myth: Crusty Old Wives

We all know at least one of those crusty old, gung-ho, esprit de corps, military men. That guy who has never married because it might interfere with his career. The guy who enjoys working late and doesn't mind making others do the same. He has a billion stripes on his sleeve and even more awards on his chest. He lives and breathes for the military. Although these men can be a pain in the ass, I don't find them nearly as obnoxious as the wives who sometimes develop the same attitude. These crusty old bags maintain that they were military wives when it was *hard*.

Her story: Her family didn't get BAH (Basic Allowance for Housing) because that'swhen family "wasn't important." They were so poor that she could not afford cleaning supplies and was forced to live in the filth of the base housing unit that only had one bedroom, despite her large family of six. She raised the kids alone. Their eldest didn't even meet his dad until he was eight!

Not only did she do this, but she *never* complained, either! (She is doing enough complaining now to make up for it though, eh?) So, she has no sympathy for you. She deserves to wear her husband's rank, because she earned it—and you, youngster, don't know how easy you have it!

Give me a break. My mother joined the military in 1984, before many of these people were married. Trust me, it hasn't changed too much. If the military really was harder (as she contends), then she must be a lot older than she looks because it hasn't changed much since the early 1900s, according to my history book.

These crusty women have been hardened by military life and they forget that they too, were once married to an entry-level enlisted man or officer. No one starts at the top. But it seems like once they get there, they forget about what it was like at the bottom. Hardship shouldn't kill compassion.

You can spot these women easily. She expects to be saluted by lower-ranking men because of who her husband is. She has no sense of humor and takes herself really damn seriously. Despite her winning personality, she has no friends. But hey, she doesn't need them. She may also volunteer to do some extra-special job and use her authority to harass you. If she takes a dislike to you, for whatever reason, you will feel the consequences of her wrath. The active military hath no fury to hold up to a crusty wife's scorn—trust me.

She is the result of a negative attitude festering over years. Notice the wrinkles and leathery skin. The best thing to do is try and avoid women like this. Don't allow her to intimidate you or pull you down to her level. If she upsets you, don't talk to her when she calls and ignore her in the commissary. What is she going to do, get your husband in trouble because his wife is unfriendly?

If you can't be a good example, you serve as a terrible warning! Consider yourself lucky if you do meet a woman like this. She will show you what the years in the military can do to someone, if she chose to be unhappy about it. It's likely that she was once bright eyed and bushy tailed, just like you are now.

Unless you want to end up like her (a smug, unhappy, old-looking, know-it-all-whom-nobody-likes), it's best to start laughing at the military now. Do things that keep you young rather than focusing on things that stress you out. Most of all, *never* take yourself or your circumstances too seriously.

Section 2: The Real Difference

Many people outside the military community tend to criticize service wives. As I have discussed before, we are sometimes classified as greedy and told that we married for the money. To repeat it, no one marries the military for money . . . only for the benefits. I wishthose gossips would get it right for once.

If you go home during a deployment, the first thing people will say to you is "I could never do that!" As if you had some choice about his deployment! They may even assume something is wrong with your marriage or that divorce is imminent.

This is a good reason why many wives grow apart from their childhood friends and grow closer to other military acquaintances. Civilians often don't understand. Keep in mind that you may have found it hard to understand before he joined as well. The military is very confusing to an outsider, as you probably know.

Since this whole book is written for wives, I have thought about the qualities I most admire about the happiest and most fun wives I know. Maybe, they have learned by trial and error, but I find the things to be true about the exceptional women I have met in the military.

I have observed all of these following qualities in the most successful women. And whether you gain these skills through this book or by making your own mistakes, I find that they are essential in the military and helpful anywhere.

Acceptance and the Air Force: The Grass Is Never Greener . . .

I have had experience in the Army, Navy and Marine Corps. This is how I came to the rather controversial conclusion that they are all the same. The Gov is excellent at making people feel like shit. Just look at the IRS. All I ever have to do when dealing with the military is think about the IRS. Then, their treatment seems to make more sense.

Many people have argued with me that all military branches are not created equal. Marines think the Army is nasty, the Army thinks Marines are too gung-ho, and neither seem to care for the Navy at all. Just ask your husband and you will get an earful about this rivalry. I am trying to illustrate the fact that things would be no different had your husband chosen to join a different service. You, as a wife, will struggle with the same things as any other military wife . . . Army, Navy, Marine or Air Force.

Maybe if he had joined a different branch, you would have a better duty station, or he would complain about uniforms less. But there would still be deployments. You would still deal with the same emotions and fears that any wife has when confronted with our nation at war. And yes, there will always be some master sergeant or colonel in charge of your husband who seems to hate him.

I see many wives wishing their husband could have joined (any other service here) because they believe things would be better. The reality is, he joined the service he joined, and now there is no escape. Wishing doesn't change it. Even if it's true that the Air Force *are* really guys in bathing suits and sunglasses who play golf

all day while your husband sweats out PT in cammies and boots—
you can't change it now. As this is a fact, there is no reason to go
through the next 4 years wishing he had made a different decision.
It's no different than wishing he hadn't joined the service at all. It
will get you nowhere and it will never make you feel better.

The best thing to do is accept the way things are. Yes, the Air
Force has bases in Myrtle Beach and Tacoma, while the Army is
stuck in Killeen, Texas. (I lovingly refer to Killeen as the armpit of
the world). And no, it is not fair! But do you want to spend your
time feeling bad, or do you want to make the best of what you
have?

The rivalry, I think, is a good thing. It builds pride in his
particular branch. This, in turn, builds men who are feeling happy
that they chose to join their service. Thinking "the Army is nasty"
is a healthy way for him to feel good about himself and his service
to this country. The happier your husband is, the less likely he is
to do a poor or careless job. Poor and careless jobs can kill in this
line of work.

Try to let go of this prejudice and make yourself just be happy
where you are. And believe me, everyone goes through this at one
time or another. The military is by nature an imperfect institution.
It is something we have to accept and deal with in the next few
years, regardless of whether we want to or not. If you chose not to
accept this, you will make yourself, your husband, your kids, and
your friends miserable with "what ifs?"

If your husband or boyfriend has not yet joined the military
and is still thinking about it, I would suggest the Air Force. It is
the only branch of the service I have no direct experience with.
Overall, though, all of the other branches seem to be jealous of
them. I have heard about how "family oriented" they are, though
I don't know how true this actually is.

If he is already in the Air Force, maybe I will be getting a
letter from you soon, telling me that I am wrong and listing all
the horrible things the Air Force has done to your husband
and family. But if you can possibly help it, please don't spoil

my hope. I would really like to believe that the Air Force is the exception to my rule.

Choosing Your Strippers, I Mean, Battles, Wisely

I once spoke to a fiancée who was in the midst of a life crisis because her soon-to-be husband wanted to go to a bachelor party with his friends at a strip bar. **She** didn't believe in that. **She** didn't like that. So **she** forbade him to go. No one bothered to ask him what **he** believed in.

To me, this seemed awfully closed-minded and un-accepting, especially since she was going to marry him. She did not respect her fiancé or trust him to make his own choices, and she made them both miserable over this nonsensical matter.

I mentioned to her that it was probably not a good idea to "forbid" a grown man to do anything. I told her that if my husband ever "forbade" me to do anything, I would probably resent him for it . . . and then do it anyway. Apparently (in her opinion), her fiancé is not as childish as I am. She was under the impression that husbands should be controlled. She also stated that her belief was that there should be absolutely *no* sexual gratification outside of marriage. To her, this included strippers. I pointed out to her that masturbation is also sexual gratification outside of marriage, but that it could not really be considered "cheating."

Almost all the military men I know engage in "loving thyself" while on deployment in order to refrain from cheating on their wives. I think it's healthy. She informed me that her husband never did that. This was the end of the conversation, as I realized that she was either majorly diluted or incredibly stupid.

There may come a time in your husband's career when he decides that he needs a night out with the guys. This might happen at a strip bar. When this occurs, I suggest you look at the real reasons behind your own feelings on this issue.

I have found that the only times I find this objectionable is when I am feeling bad about my own body, or when I am angry with my husband for another reason. When I was 9 months pregnant, for instance, I did not care for the idea one bit. (I also did not care for ice cream, and that alone should tell you how irrational I was.)

While some men may think that going to strip bars is morally wrong, I have never met one who really thought so. So (chances are) if your husband thinks this, he is either lying to you, or he is in this very, very miniscule minority. (But please don't kid yourself.) If both of you sincerely share the same beliefs on this issue, that is fantastic.

For the rest of us, I have seen many marriages (especially military marriages) fall apart over such petty arguments. I have also seen women ignoring proof of their husband's infidelity while arguing with him about nonsense issues.

In reality, neither of them accomplish anything because they refuse to deal with the *real* problems at hand. Rather than talking about how he contracted STD while on deployment, they talk about how many nights a week he works late, or if he should be "allowed" to go to a strip bar.

If you trust your husband, you should have no problems with him going out to a strip bar once in a while. Try and keep in mind that, even if you don't agree with it, you aren't the one doing it. Why should you forbid your husband, another adult, to do anything? You are not his mother and you don't want to be. Do you?

If it would really put your mind at ease, why not join him on his adventure to the strip club? It's not as bad as you imagine. Besides, I have met few men who actually cheated with strippers.

The moral of this story is to choose your battles wisely. You will never have your husband completely until he gets out of the military. You do not have the luxury of fighting and having him there every morning to make up with you. Don't dilute yourself with ownership; the military owns him. You will never own him.

You certainly do not want to alienate him to the point where he goes out *just* to get away from you. Mostly, you do not want to end up divorced over this. If you do, you can't value your husband too much. Discuss the things that really *do* matter in your relationship. Your marriage will be longer and happier for it.

Remember that it's not the military that causes divorce, it's you blaming them for causing a divorce. The military just separates families once in a while, but they don't condone divorce. Just ask them!

Hope for the Best; Prepare for Disaster

When my friend's husband was scheduled to go on a deployment shortly before Thanksgiving, it was only supposed to last for one month. She (and many other wives of the men on this deployment) decided that since their husbands would be home before Christmas, they would remain on the base and await the scheduled day. Not only did they end up spending Thanksgiving alone, but also Christmas, New Year's, and Valentine's Day. This one-month deployment ended up lasting almost 5 months. Up until Christmas day, rumors continue to fly that the men would be home before the big holiday. These rumors were started by the command.

The command did not know when to expect them home any more than the wives did. As the wives continued to harass them, so they continued to make up return days to quiet the questions. As a result, rumors about the deployment's return date flew constantly until the day the husbands finally showed up, four months later than originally planned. You will hear a lot of rumors like these. You will hear things about husbands being unfaithful during the separation. You will see the days on your calendar come and go, and you will be disappointed over and over until you don't expect to ever see him again.

Once in a great while, he may return early, but this is little consolation when he returns late. Never *ever* believe what the military says or anything else you hear, even if it comes from your husband. He doesn't know anything except for the circulating rumors where he is. The pretense of any kind of schedule is scoff-able at best.

I think the military would do best to be honest with wives about the exact day. But the truth of the matter is, they won't do it and they probably never will. But I don't think they will admit the truth . . . sometimes, *they* don't even know!

Never expect your husband to come home until you see him. Don't be crossing days off on your calendar, because you may find yourself gravely disappointed if he does not show up at the end of your countdown. The military is a bona fide madness factory. Really, the only thing you can count on from them is more of the same old, same old. That is why it works best not to believe anything until you see it. Be cautious about anything you believe in, sign, or hear about. Don't take anything at face value until you see it yourself in person or on paper, with the president's signature.

Don't presume to make any plans around a particular date. By all means, go home to your parents, if that's what you want, and don't worry about the "date of arrival." Expect nothing and you may be pleasantly surprised; expect anything solid and you are looking for disappointment.

Who Are You Calling a Dependent?

You will find that the military has a word for spouses. The word is "dependent." Personally, I don't care for this word at all. It implies something that is simply not true, for if all military wives were truly "dependent," the servicemen would be incapable of doing their jobs. Of course what the military is implying by this word is not what they believe. They consider you dependent on him for money and benefits, and that is all. They consider you *their* dependent, or in other words, *their* pain in the ass.

Obviously, they have less attachment to you than they do to your husband. You are simply another mouth to feed who comes with him. This may be unflattering, but it is how they feel. You want the truth, right?

Memorize your husband's social security number. You might as well forget your own because the Gov will never ask you for it. To them, you are him (except not deployable), and that makes you useless to them. Your individuality is certainly not important, despite the fact that you are so wonderful. As for being "dependent," that's as far as it goes.

There is nothing more annoying than a military wife who actually is "dependent." We all miss our husbands and want him with us to share in our lives all the time. But life must continue while he is gone, especially if you have kids.

Military wives are living proof that women can function capably without men. We handle the finances, the household, the shopping, and the child rearing. We are both mothers and fathers—because while he is away, we are single parents.

It is also our responsibility to catalog lost time for the men in our lives and make sure his morale is up by sending pictures and care packages. This is a job for a superwoman, not a dependent woman. There is no room for dependence, there is only room for *in*dependence. The truly dependent wife is often on some sort of antidepressant. This is okay if they keep her functional. But sometimes, they become just another excuse.

Seems like everyone struggles with bouts of depression during their lifetime, and it is really easy to be sad while your husband is away. Although this is not a pleasurable experience, it can be dealt with maturely and usually, without a crutch.

There is no need to cry hysterically and make a scene when your husband is leaving. Remember, other wives' husbands are leaving too; no one is feeling bad for you in particular. It is not helpful to badmouth his superiors for any reason unless they do something to you personally. (Sending your husband on deployment does not count.) The house should not fall to chaos while he is gone, and you should have money to spare. Wives who are truly dependent make us all look irresponsible and feel embarrassed, That is a stereotype that doesn't fit most of us. At least, I'd like to think so.

I propose that the military stop calling us "dependents." They are contributing to this stereotype and that's not "politically correct" enough for me. I believe we should be called "independents" or even given a special name like "Personal Headquarters Commanders (PHC Smith?)."

I think that I could handle this title because I have never lived up to the title of "dependent." Of course, once the Marine Corps establishes this title, I would, no doubt, be asked for my sponsor's SSN.

The most functional wives do not think of themselves as "dependents." They do not function dependently. If you are "dependent" and feel that your husband is *vital* to your survival, get over it quickly. If you don't, the military will force you to get over it. It won't be pleasant.

Patience: It's Not As Easy As It Sounds

My husband comes home after I have spent the entire day cleaning the house and says, "The house looks nice, babe." He then proceeds to the kitchen, dirties some dishes and leaves them there in the sink. He moves on to the bedroom, taking off his uniform, leaving it in a crumpled pile on the floor. He removes his underwear and misses the hamper. He gets into the shower (I don't know *what* they do in there, water polo or something?), and splashes water all over everything in the bathroom. He shaves in the sink and forgets to rinse it out.

Everywhere he goes, he leaves a dirty trail of evidence. You can literally see the aftermath of my husband's homecoming by looking at the trail of dirty cast-offs in my house. I am a slave to counterwiping and vacuuming, not to mention picking up clothes and dishes! One week before a big holiday event, my husband was preparing his gear for an inspection. This included doing God-knows-what with his boots to get them shiny. Not only does this require boot polish, but also a black, paint-like substance called "edge dressing." In my home, it is not used frequently because every time it's opened, it ends up on our carpet. My husband was having trouble opening it and decided that it needed to be heated in order to soften the paint inside the rim of the cap. He made motions towards my brand-new microwave.

I tried to stop him, but he insisted upon it. Being physically unable to stop him, he got his way. The edge dressing went into the microwave for a total of three horrible seconds as I waited for an explosion to ensue. After the three agonizing seconds, my husband removed the edge dressing from the microwave. Everything was fine! I began walking back into the kitchen just as my husband was opening the bottle carefully over the sink. Ppsshhhhhhhhzzzzzzz!!! The edge dressing had exploded as he opened it! Being an engineer, you'd think he could have predicted that.

The paint dried on contact all over the white kitchen. There were little black speckles and spots all over the floor, the counter, the sink, the walls, and everything else within reach. My kitchen was destroyed.

Our attempts at cleaning the paint seemed futile, and we soon gave up and went to bed. He never did use the damn edge dressing on his boots. I awoke in the morning with a feeling of impending doom. Because my husband was at work, it was my responsibility to get the kitchen cleaned up before the holiday party at my home that weekend.

I decided three things: The first, I needed paint thinner and had none. Secondly, I had to start early if there was any hope of restoring my kitchen that day. Lastly, I made a mental note to kill my husband. I began calling my network of friends. They were all wives, but none of them had cars that day.

I ended up having to call an acquaintance, who (luckily) had both a car and some paint thinner and was willing to help me clean up after my idiot husband's accident. She arrived loaded with all the appropriate gear. After an hour of work, we had restored one square foot of my kitchen floor. The fumes in the kitchen were overcoming us and she suggested that she do the cleaning while I went elsewhere, since I was pregnant. I refused her offer but invited her to my holiday party for the kind thought.

After we had scrubbed for the entire day, we had the kitchen looking halfway normal again. My husband arrived home just in time to see us mopping up the floor with bleach. We were tired, hungry, headachy, and exceedingly unhappy with *him*.

After noting our progress, he commented, "Wow, babe, the kitchen looks nice. I am going to grab a bite and take a shower. I am so tired." He proceeded to leave another trail through my now clean house. Ahhhhh!!!!

Will this happen to you? Maybe not. But we all have some story that is comparable. No matter what you believe about your lovely husband, you will find him annoying at times. As it is not always easy to not "sweat the small stuff," a good amount of patience is also required.

Try and refrain from killing him and you may have a happy life together. By losing your temper, you lose control, and nothing will get done if *you* lose control!

Dreams Have No Location

If you heed but one warning in this book, please heed this one, for it is something that I have the most regret about. College is something we all consider at some point. Many choose not to go and that's okay. I myself did not make a conscious choice not to go. Rather, I continued to postpone it until I realized that I could have already graduated.

Military couples often choose to marry because of two factors: money and location. Location is important because many couples would like to remain together throughout their courtship and the military makes this hard with the inevitable deployments and moves. A couple will decide to live together rather than be separated by states, or even countries. However, this presents a problem with pay because the military does not pay a man enough to live on his own unless he is married or high ranking. Although the money when married is not a big difference, it can be a deciding factor. A little more money is better than none. So it is also a good idea (financially) to be married, if you decide that you absolutely cannot live without each other for the next four years.

All the women I have met who are married and not currently in college seem to have an excuse about why college is not possible. My excuse was that I wanted to go to a university. I was too smart for the local community college. Besides, I thought that we would be moving any day now.

After almost 4 years in the same place, that community college has started looking pretty damn good! It has become obvious to me that I must not have been as smart as I thought and perhaps, the community college was for me after all.

However, excuses are just that. While they may be valid excuses, they are excuses all the same. When you are done giving excuses, you are no more educated than you were before. Don't be stuck-up about college, or any dream you may have. As soon as you land at your husband's duty station, go to the first college you see and sign up for all university-level transferable classes. You may still lose some when you move, but you will not have lost the knowledge, the most important thing.

If you have children, take night classes or find out about day care. You can even get a friend to watch them for you in exchange for watching her kids on weekends. All of these excuses can be worked out if you want college (or any dream) badly enough.

After my husband's four years of service (and three years of marriage), I am no closer to my goal of becoming a doctor. Although I have learned much about life, love, marriage, parenting, and living as a military wife, these skills are highly unmarketable. The biggest thing I have learned is not to stop following your dreams for the benefit of others. Although I love my family, I find it hard not to resent them for my own mistake. I chose to give up these 4 years and I am not sorry for what I have accomplished so far. I just know I could have accomplished more.

I hope now that I can convince you of the same thing, maybe preventing someone else from postponing her dreams. If college is not one of your goals, okay! But there are other goals and dreams.

Although the military can complicate the road to any goals, do not allow it to squelch the possibility. No one can hold you back from your dreams but yourself.

Growing Where You're Planted

"Growing where you are planted" is much easier said than done. The most successful wives I know are the ones who have this concept down and practice it. *It is essential.* Take comfort in the fact that you can be happy, no matter where you may be and under any circumstances. You too can choose to enjoy and even love the diversity that life in the military can offer to you.

Take every opportunity to make friends wherever you are, and your loneliness will subside. Building a life for yourself has nothing to do with your location. I have learned this lesson over and over again. Whether introducing yourself to a neighbor, volunteering, or attending company picnics, you can find an opportunity wherever you may be. What you create in your many (or few) homes is entirely up to you. Whether you want to spend this time longing for better circumstances or living your life is also up to you. But choose wisely, for life is too short to slump around in a perfectly good planter. So grow up!

I DID NOT OVERREACT!

When I was eight months pregnant, I discovered that my wedding ring no longer fit on my chubby fingers. I compromised by putting it on a chain that I wore around my neck. I began to fidget with it frequently. One day, when I instinctively began to reach for it, I couldn't find it! I had lost my wedding ring!

My hormones raged out of control and I began to sob uncontrollably. My husband was upset too—before he pointed out to me that the chain was still around my neck. It had gotten lost between my many pregnancy-induced chin folds. Feeling a bit stupid, my only recourse was to sigh over my relative state of fatness. This is a great example of getting upset over something small. A wedding ring *is* a big deal to most of us, but it's not worth a heart attack. In the end, it was not such a big problem after all.

In my case, everyone was in hysterics for a few minutes, all because I failed to think the situation through calmly and gather complete information. By overreacting, I scared my husband, myself, and probably the poor baby too.

Remember that you are the "wo-man with the plan". You set

the tone in the family, no matter what you allow your husband to believe. There would be chaos in your family without you. With that in mind, remember how much your attitude will affect others. If you are cool and have everything together, chances are that your family will too. As a leader, your challenge is to be calm and rational. Split-second decisions may be necessary, but that is no reason to be unprepared for them. If you cannot control yourself and your reactions, your family may remain in hysterics for the next 4 years. You need to be capable of making choices that are in the best interests of the entire family.

Being emotional is completely normal. You cannot be blamed or faulted for being upset once in a while or for crying yourself to sleep now and then. The truth is, we are not superwomen. We have a hard job and we are all trying to cope as best we can. We are all emotional at times and it *is* allowed.

The ability to deal with your emotions is what makes you strong, compared to your husband. It is what makes you capable of controlling yourself. Being a woman is a strength, not a weakness. Have faith in yourself and the rest will fall into place. Don't change who you are. Do not allow the military to change who you are. I am certain that your husband married you because he loves the person that you are. He feels confident that you will be able to tackle this challenge. You should feel confident too. Let the person you are shine through no matter what the circumstances, and the years are sure to fly by.

Q & A

Q. I know my way pretty good around the Navy, but now, I have an Army guy . . . what's the difference?

A. They wear different uniforms and the Navy has more ships. That's about it. Actually, that is the only difference between the Navy and all of the branches, so you are set!

Q. He was telling me that he has to talk to some financial advisor for the Air Force about marrying me. Can they tell him no?

A. Um, yes! They can tell him whatever they want. Can they stop him from marrying you? No.

Q. Sometimes, other wives talk down to me because Brian is enlisted. I don't like that and I don't know how to respond.

A. Remind them that you are not in the military here, and neither are they. You see, in the civilian world, we don't go by rank, we go by who can kick the most ass. (Note: If you say this, you should feel confident that you can, in fact, kick her ass.)

Q. How do you handle this constant frustration of not knowing even the tiniest bit of what the future holds?

A. I forgot that when my husband was a civilian, I had psychic powers that always told me what the future holds! Until they come back when he is a civilian again, I would say that the small things count. I know that he will be getting up at o'dark-thirty for the rest of his enlistment. That's a tiny bit of knowledge about the future, right?

Foreword: An Amusing Tale from Behind the Lines

(by Mia, Camp LeJeune)

One day, my husband came home and asked me to do him a big favor. I, the doting wife, readily agreed without knowing what it was that he needed. He went on to tell me a sob story about a company PT that was planned the next day.

He said that they were going to have to run 8 miles and then do an obstacle course. I said sorry, but I still did not know what he wanted me to do about it. I soon found out. He asked me to incapacitate him so that he didn't have to do it. I was taken aback. He wanted me to smash his toe with a hammer. I gaped at him in horror. I was horrified. "No," I said, "I refuse to purposely hurt you so that you don't have to run."

He begged and pleaded until I was so fed up with him that I wanted to do bodily harm. So I told him to go and get the hammer. When he gave me the hammer and I bent down to look at his toe, I started to sob uncontrollably. I could not make myself hurt my beloved husband and his unsuspecting toe.

I really tried, but every time I brought the hammer up to smash his toe, I just cringed with horror and contempt. I couldn't do it. So my husband got another bright idea. He suggested I stand on a chair and drop the hammer on his toe. Okay, at least then I wouldn't be face-to-face with his innocent toe. So I got up on the chair and started to take aim. I took a good amount of time aiming because I did not want to miss.

I guess I didn't aim well enough because when the hammer dropped, it started to fall at an angle and ended up forked-edge down. It also had veered forward so that it just grazed the very top of his nail. It was obvious that I had failed miserably.

He screamed like a girl and announced that I broke it. I told him to quit being a baby and that I should do it again to make sure I broke it. I was feeling a little sadistic at that point. He said no and made me drive him to the ER.

After a few hours, when the doctor finally came around, he asked what happened. We informed him that a hammer had fallen from a high place and hit him on the toe. I wasn't about to add lying to my many sins.

The doctor looked at it and told us that it was just bruised. But he did put a little hospital booty on it and gave him the infamous, all-healing Motrin.

After we left the hospital, we had to make a stop at his squad leader's house to tell him what happened so that he could get out of the PT. When the squad leader opened the door, I noticed that he had a bandaged ankle.

After he finished talking and limped back to our vehicle, I asked him what had happened to his leader. Evidentially, he had fallen down his steps and twisted his ankle. I thought that he probably asked his wife to push him.

If that wasn't bad enough, when my husband went to work the next day, he found that the CO had gotten into a car accident the night before and broke his leg. So nobody had to PT at all.

I just thought it was amusing that these tough men, these guardians of our country, were doing bodily harm to themselves to get out of running. I bet the CO's wife was driving the car and he had asked her to crash it. I wouldn't doubt it, knowing about all the little "accidents" that had befallen these poor men.

CHAPTER 4

A Guide to Your Government-Issued Husband

Your husband has chosen a very noble career path for himself. No matter what his motivation for joining, it's probably not all that he expected.

Many women are shocked the first time they are reunited with their significant others after boot camp or school. Sometimes, a deployment or a float brings home a completely different man wearing your husband's uniform. Many find that their husbands have undergone complete makeovers in the attitude department. Their sensitive husbands have somehow been assaulted by military life. He may have picked up swearing, become more or less religious, become more outspoken . . . or not. He could be cleaner, messier, fatter, thinner, or more polite. You never know.

We tend to forget that people *always* change over time when confronted with such things. When we don't see them for several months, this change may seem more pronounced because we have not been given the time to get used to it. Even if your husband is the most predictable guy ever, the military causes people to change. Remember, ladies, boot camp is not a charm school. I can hardly imagine that one learns to be a gentleman on a naval ship or in a barracks. Drastic lifestyle changes like these tend to bring out some strange reactions in even the strongest of men.

In the interest of humor and to remedy some of the shock for you, I have prepared a rather lengthy list of things that he may or may not pick up. I am of the opinion that the military should publish a government handbook containing such information. However, I guess they would deem my version inappropriate.

Whatever the case may be, here are my observations of servicemen (after), for better or for worse, till death do you part.

Things you need to know about operating your new husband:

On Sleep. Your husband loves sleep. He has acquired this great appreciation during boot camp. It will last at least until he gets out of the military. If your husband is like mine, he is virtually impossible to wake during his slumber.

Never, and I repeat, *never*, try and wake him while he is sleeping. If you find that you must wake him, be sure to use a very, very long stick. This may seem like a hassle until you see the "waking reaction" that occurs. Some men have been known to strangle their wives during this waking process. Although you probably won't die, he may still take a swing at you.

On Paranoia. The military man is always ready for war; he looks for it everywhere. It is what he has trained for. He eats, sleeps, breathes, thinks, and lives for war! Obnoxious as this may seem, the thinking part is what is really intrusive to a serene lifestyle. He may tell you not to or to post family photos on the Internet. He may try to tell you that your phone is tapped, or that he is being followed.

I never understood why my husband thought these things, until one day I read his "terrorism awareness" manual. It talked about how to outrun a terrorist and how to check a package for bombs. When I was through reading that manual, I watched my back for days. Don't believe me? Go ahead, read it. Then imagine being brainwashed with this kind of information daily.

You will soon sympathize with those old "crazy" guys who set booby traps in their back yards and live all alone with fear. After all, if he stays in the military, that might well be your husband some day!

On Cleaning. Make no mistake, your man is a very clean person . . . at work. When he gets home, however, get ready for the messes to occur. After all, he has been cleaning at work all day, right? Why should he have to come home and pick up after himself? That's ridiculous! When I got married, I liked the fact that my husband was a neatness freak. For him, everything had to be spotless and there could be no clutter. It wasn't until after we were married that I noticed that *I* was the one making sure that everything was up to the military standard.

I have never seen one of these men scrub a toilet in their own home or do anything else that may remotely qualify as "cleaning." I have, however, heard criticism about how my cleaning is "unsat" (unsatisfactory).

On "showing you a couple of moves." Don't let this happen. He may try to manipulate you into thinking that he is teaching you something useful in case you are attacked. Really, what he is doing is practicing his moves on you. He will say that he is not going to hurt you, but don't trust that. Not your gentle husband? Wait for it!

There you will be, lying on the floor and cradling your painful injury and staring up at him in surprise and betrayal. Ouch.

On Movies. You don't want to see a movie with your husband. Do not make friends with military personnel and take them out to see a movie. If there is even a hint of anything military in the movie whatsoever, it will be scrutinized until you lose your sanity.

Just know that you will not be watching the remainder of the movie after some guy in a uniform comes on. Your husband feels responsible for telling you about everything that happens to be "wrong" with the uniform, the salute, or even his bearing. These men turn into yapping dogs during these films and this kind of behavior begs to be extinguished. If you learn how to do this, let me know.

Mistakes Are Not Tolerated. Do not ever confuse any other branch of the military with your husband's. He will take it as a great insult, and he could divorce you over it. This is the most unforgivable insult to his military persona. You have to remember that his branch of the military is the BEST and most "manly." Always and forever, amen. God bless his branch . . . and *only* his branch!

Big Is Beautiful. No, I'm not talking about *your* weight! His plan is to scare the enemy with his sheer size and manliness. Don't be surprised if he wants to spend a lot of time in the gym or drink weird milk shakes. Heaven help your peace if he loses even one pound.

They are in the military, so they must *look* like they are in the military. If this proves impossible, they would like to look like bodybuilders instead. Remember, ladies, always tell them that they "look big to you," even if you aren't in the bedroom. Oh, and Arnold is a wussy, too!

On Illness. They seem to be prone to it. Indeed, he will contract every disease known to man, from poison oak to malaria. Not only are they prone to it, they are big weenies about it, too. They will lie in bed for days on end and torture you mercilessly, requesting any childish thing that they can think of.

You better hope your four-year-old gets sick before he does. And make sure to always buy him the Nyquil *caplets* because the syrup hurts his throat. So your big, bad soldier has a hangnail, huh? I'll be sure and send a get-well-soon card for you because by the time he is well, you won't be.

Beware of Brainwashing. He may be your little cuddly bear when he gets on the plane to boot camp, but expect someone brand new when he returns. In boot camp, they are programmed to "kill, kill, kill." So when he comes to give you that long-awaited "hello hug," it's really a chokehold.

They have erased the word "love" from his vocabulary, for a while, at least. His smile muscles have vanished and have been replaced with an automatic snarl. It will take a while for him to work his mouth back up to a smirk. Oh, and don't be confused when you hear "yes ma'am" instead of your name . . . that is his new name for you, and all others like you. It may not seem that bad at first, but it will get tiresome over time. Don't worry, being with you 24-7 for the next month might get him back to normal. Too bad he has to go to combat training now, huh? So more "kill, kill, kill"—sorry, ladies. But you'll have him back in four years. Start buying Tylenol in bulk in the meantime.

On Cheating, all military wives are considered "cheaters." You will have to continually fight this reputation. Even if your husband doesn't really believe you are a cheater, all his single friends will try to convince him that you are while he is on deployment. This is part of the male brotherhood campaign to enlist him to join their "single guy" activities. It's the old, "Well, she does it to *you*, my man." It is considered fair play. These other men believe that being single makes them the gurus of all relationships, don't you know? And the gurus say, "Women cheat." Whatever else you do, don't prove them right. He will still be painfully surprised if you *do* cheat on him and your marriage will suffer.

Defining "work day." You may think that your husband is doing some incredibly stressful stuff while at work. You are right, to a point. Their stress lasts for about an hour a day. They spend this hour getting yelled at, PTing, being inspected, and playing soldier. The remainder of their 13-hour day is spent on complicated tasks such as beating others at Playstation, watching pornos, comparing wives, belittling each other, napping, practicing "moves" on each other, you know . . . studly man stuff. Then he comes home and says in a sarcastic tone, "What have *you* been doing all day?" Tell him that you have been really busy playing on the Playstation!

On Beer. This is what your paycheck is for. Evidently, beer is their only antidepressant. It is also his only motivation to make it through the incredibly stressful workday. Expect to be alone on the weekends sometimes. His friends expect him to spend even more time with them, drinking beer and discussing Playstation! They have to hang together. This is male-bonding business.

On Food. Food will become especially important. Try not to get too grossed out when he describes to you some horrible concoction that he consumed while in the field. Food will also be especially appreciated when he returns from boot camp. Don't be too surprised when he cooks canned foods by placing them directly onto the stove or tries other outlandish things. You may think he is attempting to burn down the house, but that is not his plan—even if he *does* start a fire.

On Hair, there are two kinds of guys: Those who miss their hair, and those who didn't have much to begin with. Either way, get ready for an earful if he sees one of those "hippies" with hair longer than his. You may not come across this much in a hardcore military town, but sooner or later, you will travel to the "real" world.

His senses may be overwhelmed when you do this. Try to be patient even if you find it trivial. Always budget for those weekly haircuts. I have seen military men get very upset because a barber "messed up" their alleged hair, so the expensive barber may be a must.

On "pig-ism" (or chauvinism). Whether your husband has been deployed for 6 months or 18 months, he has been away from you for a long time (especially in guy years). Also, keep in mind he has been residing on a ship, barracks, or possibly a tent. He has shared these residences with others like him, only single.

So, when he finally returns to you, expect him to refer to you as "woman" for a while. He will commit other social taboos that may be uncharacteristic of him. Don't worry, he will get over it as long as his friends aren't around. But remember, all your hard work and training goes straight down the toilet the next time he is deployed.

On Vocabulary, or "military lingo." Many wives find this frightening and incomprehensible. Husbands come home from boot camp talking another language. Most of this lingo is abbreviation. He will laugh at you when you ask what "NVG" means, but don't be afraid, after all, he is your husband! He is just experimenting with being bilingual.

About the Phone. You will learn that he fears it. Your husband does not want to answer the phone. That is your job because you are the secretary. And by the way, he is "not home," unless it is someone he wants to talk to. So you need to know who he may wish to speak to before he does. In other words, you are a mind reader.

He does not want to answer the phone because it might be work. Just because he has only been home for 14 minutes does not mean that they cannot—or will not—call him back. And he is tired. Many military wives screen their phone calls with an answering machine. If you do not have an answering machine, you are going to *be* the answering machine!

"Vitamin M": You may hear your husband referring to this. You may not yet know what it is, but you will soon! "Vitamin M" stands for Motrin. Motrin is the military's super-excellent wonder drug. Really, it is the best the Gov has. Be aware that your husband has already ingested more Motrin than you can possibly fathom. He is completely immune to it (or so he says).

Just know that your husband could break his leg, have his bone protruding from his skin, and they would prescribe Motrin. He would go to the medic or the doctor and the doctor would be telling the same thing, "Take Motrin for the pain and stay hydrated. It'll be okay in a couple of days."

About Cars. He wants one. A nice one. These men are possessed to think they deserve to drive a Mercedes SUV. Although the vehicle he wants may be far from reasonable, there is little you can do to stop him from resisting the temptation.

If you do, he might carpool with his friends to avoid being seen in your reasonable piece of junk. Either that, or he will spend thousands of dollars on stereo equipment and a chrome finish for it so it can look like a dressed-up piece of reasonable junk. Either way, you will end up spending more than your military budget can afford on.

On Swearing. He does it . . . a lot. He might even pass it on to you, like a disease. You will be talking to your mother when she mentions to you that you just used the "f" word 6 times in the last sentence. You won't remember this. Just start to think of the word "fuck" as a descriptive word like "stupid" or even a transition word like "and." Your mother might even get used to the swearing.

On Tattoos. He must have one. All of his friends have one, so he needs one too. They are also considered a right of passage into the military. If your husband does not want to engage in this childish behavior, congratulations!

If he does, there is no way to convince him that he does not need his social security number tattooed on his chest in case he loses his dog tags. One strategy to keep it from happening is to tell him you don't have the money. When you think about it, it's not a lie!

On Being Passive. He will do it with his buddies, the command, the grocery store, etc. It's annoying as hell, too. When it comes to his career, he will take something someone tells him as golden and not question it further. Then, he will come home and give you the same load of bullshit that someone at work gave him. And he will expect you to believe it.

When you ask him if he said something, he will say no and refuse to deal with the situation further. You are not allowed to say anything to anyone about his career. If he is too passive to stand up for himself, you're just going to have to sit back and wait for things to happen . . . like he does.

A Clean Shave is a necessity. You might believe that since your husband shaved regularly *before* he got into the military, it's no problem! Maybe he is even one of those lucky men who don't have to shave quite as frequently. Unfortunately, being told that he *must* shave will make him long for the days when he didn't have to (even though he did). This results in him moaning and groaning at you about his poor face.

Last Names. You will never know his buddies' first names. You may hear them, but mostly, you will refer to them as you hear them referred to. Your husband is the only exception, trusting that you already know his first name. If your husband finds his name particularly embarrassing, it may be in your best interests not to use it around his buddies. Or, if you are like me, you might choose to torture him (and invite his friends to do the same) by addressing him by his first name, frequently, and in public.

None of his friends know his first name and have always known him by his last name. If a man calls and gives his first name, you will not know who he is until he gives you the last name as well. It is astoundingly fun to play the "What's your first name?" game at military gatherings. Like middle names are in the civilian world, first names in the military are generally unknown. By the way, your name will be "Sgt. Johnson's wife." Welcome to the military!

War Cries. You may hear them a lot (or not at all), depending on his motivation level and pride in his service. The Marines are especially good at this. "Oorah!" "Hoorah!" "Hooah!" No matter how you say it, it all sounds like a grunt to me! However, each service has a unique motivation call.

My husband forced me to learn this and coaxed me to say it frequently, and still does. "Oorah!" is a frequently uttered phrase in our home. It can mean anything from "Affirmative," to "Goodbye," to "Wow."

If you have seen the show *Home Improvement*, you will recognize these interesting battlecries. They are very similar to the grunting of Tim Allen. I can only hope that my daughter does not pick this up permanently.

Green. Get use to the color—everything he owns will be green. Your house will be virtually filled with green junk. I suggest buying a house with an extra bedroom to camouflage all this green gear. If you are not lucky enough to have an extra bedroom, your closets and dressers will overflow with green.

The novelty of this bona fide gear will soon wear away, leaving you with a house full of useless stuff to hide. Unless green and camouflage matches your home decor, find some big tubs and a deep, dark closet. If you successfully hide these eyesores, please let me know how you did it. I still cannot seem to keep the cammies in the closet.

The only comfort is that my friends are all military wives so they expect nothing less when they call. It also gives us an attractive target for ridicule and complaint.

He Overcomes. I would have never thought to change the baby's diaper with a gas mask on, ever! It just never crossed my mind. One day, I recognized the familiar smell and told my husband it was his turn to change her.

When I heard her terrified cries, I rushed into the room to find my husband changing her diaper. A soiled and stinky mess it was, after all. My husband had donned his gas mask and he grinned widely at me over the child's frightened screams. "This is not so bad, babe! I don't know what the big deal is about changing dirty diapers!"

I don't pretend to know how they come up with this stuff, but husbands usually find a way to cope with difficult situations in a creative manner. In doing this, they do sometimes frighten others. You have been warned.

On Uniforms. They must be ironed and sharp looking at all times. My husband seems to think that ironing is a girly job. Whatever his argument, don't ever allow him to teach you to iron or polish boots. You *will* regret it. After you have mastered these skills, it will become your job forever.

On Dog Tags. Don't touch them. Ever. Especially when he's just gotten out of boot camp. "When they come off him, it means he is dead." And by the way, if he is a Marine, he cannot die without permission. Interesting thought, huh?

"This recruit requests permission to die, Drill Sergeant!" No one is asking you to understand, just to know. And don't touch the damn dog tags!

What Did He Say?

This is all too familiar. My husband arrives home, eager to tell me about his day and to know about mine: something common among married couples (I assume). I don't have any problems telling him what I did, but when it's his turn, I have little enthusiasm. I sit back in my seat, my eyes glaze over with a monotone "a huh" drifting from my lips. I hear nothing and I understand even less.

No matter what your husband does for the military, you may find that you understand little about it. Not that you aren't interested, but it is nearly impossible to keep up with his story due to the barrage of military jargon that will inevitably hinder your communication. Night vision goggles become NVGs. A bunk inspection will be a JOB. He will use words such as "flack" and "kevlar." There are thousands of them. And if your husband is in the Navy, it will be even more challenging. Even the other branches of the military don't understand Navy jargon!

He carries on for a while before he interrupts himself, "You're not listening to me!" Despite your protests, you will not be able to convince him that you are listening . . . because in truth, you aren't. You can't repeat a single word he said.

It is essential for your husband to vent his frustrations so that he can wake up early tomorrow and endure another day. Tackle this communication problem so that he doesn't simply vent it *on* you.

The best method is simply to tell him *before* he begins to talk that you don't understand what he is saying because the jargon is unfamiliar to you. He should be able to understand that and start leaving the jargon at work to speak English at home. If your husband is like mine, he may take it upon himself to translate everything into English so that you are "learning something." Either way, you will understand better if you just speak up. You will inevitably pick up some military terminology and begin using it. The military subculture, for whatever reason, uses a different language from what the common folk in America do.

Someday, you too will "make a head call" or even "swab a deck." This language also includes several colorful swear words which I will not go into detail about . . . I trust you will begin to hear them soon enough.

I have compiled a limited list of jargon. These are the most frequently used. Keep in mind that whole books could be written on the subject of military jargon, so this list is far from complete. Every day, there are new ones and at times, I myself have to ask what this or that stands for. You are not expected to know all these things. So learn away only if you dare (or if you care).

Frequently-Used Nonsense (Jargon)

AAFES—Army and Air Force Exchange Service
AAR—After Action Report
AFB—Air Force Base
AFSC—Air Force Specialty Code, A job, see MOS
AIREVAC—Airborne evacuation
AIT—Advanced Individual Training
AMC—Air mobility Command

AQL—Acceptable Quality Level

ARC—Alcoholism Rehabilitation Center

AUNK—Army, rank Unknown

AWOL—Absence Without Leave

Aye—Yes (or) understood

BAH—Basic Allowance for housing barracks—Living spaces on base or post—see quarters

BAS—Basic Allowance for Sustenance

BCGs—Birth Control Glasses

BCT—Basic Combat Training

BEQ—Bachelor Enlisted Quarters

BDU—Battle Dress Uniform

BMC—Base Medical Center

BMO—Battalion Maintenance Officer

BMR—Basic Military Requirements brig—A jail or prison for military personnel bulkhead—The wall

CAT—Command Assessment Team

CDR—Contractor Discrepancy Report

CFO—Chief Finance Officer

CHAMPUS—Civilian Health and Medical Programs of the Uniformed Services (What we had before TRICARE, see TRICARE)

CIF—Central Issue Facility

CO—Commanding Officer

COLA—Cost of living Allowance con-leave—Convalescent leave

CONUS—Continental United States court martial—In the service, a military court of law deck—The floor

DEERS—Defense Enrollment Eligibility Reporting System deploy—To send ships and personnel abroad for duty

DEW—Distant Early Warning (system)

DITY—Do it yourself Move

DNIF—Duties Not Including Flying

DOD—Department of Defense

DOR—Date of Rank

DPV—Desert Patrol Vehicle

EAM—Emergency Action Message

EAS, EAOS—End of Active Obligated Service

ELS—Expected Loss of Service

ELT—Emergency Locator Transmission

EOD—Explosive Ordnance Disposal (Team)

EOS—End of Obligated Service

ERB—Emergency Radio Beacon

ETS—End of Term in Service

EWS—Electronic Warfare System

GI—A slang word, "Government Issued" or "Government Inspected"

GMO—General Medical Officer

GQ—General Quarters (aboard ship) galley—A shipboard kitchen

GITMO—Guantanamo Bay, Cuba (U.S. Naval/Marine Station)

GMT—Greenwich Mean Time (see Zulu) guidon—A company identification pennant

HAWC—Health and Wellness Center head—The bathroom; see latrine

HUEY—A type of helicopter

Humvee—All-terrain vehicle, replacing the Jeep.

JAG—Judge Advocate General

JOB—Junk on Bunk (for inspection)

JRTC—Joint Readiness Training latrine—The bathroom; see head

LES—Leave and Earning Statement

Leavenworth—The brig, Ft. Leavenworth, see brig

LOR—Letter of Reprimand

MARS—Military Affiliate Radio System

MATS—Military Air Transport Service

MCAS—Marine Corps Air Station

MCRD—Marine Corps Recruit Depot

MEB—Medical Evaluation Board

MEDEVAC—Aeromedical Evacuation

MOS—Military Occupational Specialty

MP—Military Police

MRE—Meals Ready to Eat

MTF—Medical Treatment Facility

MWR—Morale, Welfare and Recreation

NADA—Naval Aviation Depot

NAS—Naval Air Station

NAVCARE—A clinic name, see TRICARE

NAVEX—NHSD beneficiaries' pharmacy

NAVSTA—Navy station

NCO—Non Commissioned Officer

NCOIC—Non Commissioned Officer in Charge

NEST—Nuclear Emergency Search Team

NHSD—Naval Hospital, San Diego

NIS—Naval Investigative Service

NMCSD—Naval Medical Center, San Diego

NTC—Naval Training Center

NUNK—Navy, rank unknown

NVG—Night Vision Goggles

OCONUS—Outside the continental United States

OIC—Officer in Charge overhead—The ceiling

P&R—Pay and Records

PCS—Permanent Change of Station

PEB—Physical Evaluation Board

POC—The Point or Person of Contact

POD—Plan of the Day

PRT—Physical Readiness Test

PTE—Prior to Enlistment quarters—Living spaces aboard a ship; see barracks rack—A bed or cot

RRS—Rate, Rank & Service

SAC—Strategic Air Command

SAR—Search and Rescue (Team)

SCR—Systems Change Request

SEAL—SEa-Air-Land (Team)

Sick Bay—A ship's "clinic"

Sick Call—A time and place where service members report for medical evaluation

SIMA—Ship's Intermediate Maintenance Activity

SIQ—Sick in Quarters

SOP—Standard Operating Procedure

SP—Shore Patrol

TAD—Temporary Assigned Duty
TDY—Temporary Duty
TRICARE—(CHAMPUS) Dependent Insurance
UA—Unauthorized Absence
UCMJ—Uniform Code of Military Justice
UDT—Underwater Demolition Team
UIC—United Identification Code
UOD—Uniform of the Day
USA—United States Army
USAF—United States Air Force
USCG—United States Coast Guard
USMC—United States Marine Corps
USN—United States Navy
USNS—United States Naval Ship (not a regular part of fleet)
USS—United States Ship
VA—Veterans Administration watch—A turn at standing watch
     on ship; a lookout
WESPAC—Western Pacific and Asia region wilco—Will comply
WWQ—Worldwide Qualified (for duty)
XO—Executive Officer
Zulu—Greenwich Mean Time (see GMT)

Your Husband's Rigggghhhts . . .

Truth # 4: *The U.S. Constitution does not apply to your husband.* He has no rights. In order to understand this, you must first understand that they control him completely. There is no complaining about how the military is mean or unfair to him in particular. It doesn't change anything, and no one feels bad for either of you.

I have heard military wives on countless occasions exclaim "They can't do this!" Yes, they can do this. They can do whatever they want because your husband *belongs* to them. You need to realize that this is nothing personal. The military treats everyone the same: as if they are disposable and don't matter. The military does not discriminate. They have no personal qualms with anyone. They are not torturing your husband because they hate him. They just torture *everyone* because it is the nature of the organization, their policy. They don't care. Your life will be much easier when you learn to accept this fact. Only four more years to go!

"Those Filthy Sailors"

I once knew a girl with a Navy boyfriend. She got extremely upset when her co-workers taunted (in fun) about her boyfriend's "other chicks."

The stereotype did not concern me as much as the girl's reaction to it. She constantly protested that she was certain he did not have a girl at every port, and that she was the only one, absolutely. Everyone else needed to believe it too! In a relationship so recently established, it would be impossible to know for sure that he did not have girls elsewhere.

She was not married to him. Even if she had been, could she still be so certain about his eternal fidelity? It seems to me that she could have laughed off all this joking with the rest of her friends and not allow it to torment her.

She was so set on convincing everyone else that her boyfriend was faithful that I began to think that she did not believe it herself. After all, why else would she care and protest so much about what others thought? Deep down, she feared that he fit the stereotype and did not want to admit it, even to herself. What started out as a harmless joke became an issue with her that she had to take a serious look at.

Sailors will always be stereotyped, along with everyone else in the military and in the world, for that matter. Stereotypes are alive and well everywhere. We need to always examine our reasons for caring so much about what others say—about our husbands and our relationships with them. Sometimes, even when you are trying to save face, you end up showing your true fears without knowing it.

Rumors and stereotypes happen. It is our reaction to them that counts.

Where Are the Grownups?

Who said that the military stifles individuality? Although the uniforms are the same, the men under them are far from it. You will find that, in essence, your husband has even more personality than before. Maybe that is the nature of humans who are forced to outwardly conform. No matter what the reasons, these men are far from being grownups. When my husband was a private, he got into trouble. He would go out doing the typical young-military-man things: drinking, getting into fights and finally, being thrown into jail. He would call the NCO, who would trudge to the jail in the middle of the night, yell at him, and take him to the barracks to sleep it off.

I think he always knew that his payback would come. But he did not foresee our marriage. I am the one who is ultimately responsible for answering the phone and deciding if the man on the other end is worthy to speak to my husband. If I make a mistake, my husband is forced to go pick someone up or sort out some other problem for a young man in his charge.

The military does not force young servicemen to take responsibility for their own actions. Instead, they force the higher ranks to be responsible for them, as if they are children. This is annoying, and it will interfere with your life at one point or another. Young servicemen are often reckless and immature. They only seem to grow up when they are forced to be responsible for the actions of another, which usually does not happen until they get promoted to the higher ranks. Of course, maturity is always a choice.

To prove this "not grown" theory to yourself, consider having a weekend barbecue and inviting some of your husband's buddies. Their youth will be obvious almost immediately. Here is how it goes at my house. The men will greet me politely and introduce themselves. They greet my husband with a friendly "Hey, shitbird!" They proceed to conversing, using words like "dude," "man," and "bro."

Any child is greeted and patted on the head. Later, there may be a good game of "horsy" in store for them. The men might then relax with a good wrestling match in the back yard (after I kick them out) and they will be fascinated with whatever is cooking on the grill outside. They will proceed to give the cook (my husband) cooking tips and lessons, usually resulting in another wrestling match.

I have watched them perform covert operations, climbing over the neighbor's fences, hunting flies, or making crank calls to their friends on duty. No doubt about it, these grown men think that they are James Bond (but more handsome, cool and dangerous).

In need of some serious entertainment, I once gave them something constructive to do. There is nothing more amusing than watching three cocky Marines attempt to put together a baby rocker.

They could surely do it; engineers, are they not? Right. I was devastated when they requested a little baggy for all the "extra parts." It only took a couple of hours. Evidentially, those baby accessories are more difficult to put together than a landmine or plane engine. Remember, these men work with explosives daily! Shudder!

At the end of the day, when everyone went home, the house was a disaster. The barbecue was dirty and my kitchen utensils were spread all over the yard. Dirt had been tracked in and out, the movies were all over the place, and the box to the baby rocker was still on the living room floor. There were also a multitude of dead insects, casualties of the fly hunt. If you think a toddler can inflict major disruption, invite three "grown" Marines for dinner. Whoo!

The Change: Needles

The closest I came to seeing any kind of active duty activity, without a doubt, was while I was incarcerated in Navy boot camp. After several days, which saw us constantly on our feet and in-processing, we were already exhausted from the rigors of boot camp life. Mostly, all we wanted to do was sleep.

We were awakened that morning at 3 A.M. to get up and get ready for the day. This was not unusual, although official reveille did not occur until around 4 A.M. We were marched across the base in our newly issued boots, wearing our recruit hats and blue

Navy sweats. Petty Officer's objective was to get us immunized before breakfast. Everything takes a long time in boot camp. The military's infamous "hurry up and wait" attitude does exist. We spent hours in that building waiting.

I myself am not particularly afraid of needles. Being raised in a military household by an Army Nurse, our vaccinations were always up to date. Here I was in Navy boot camp, getting stuck in waiting by the Gov once again.

I waited what seemed like forever with my fellow recruits for my turn to go through the vaccination line. I was issued a plastic card that was strung onto my dog tag chain. I began going through the assembly line of needles. Two medics immediately asked me, "Are you allergic to . . ." As soon as I gave a negative response, they both promptly injected me, one in each arm. Needless to say, my arms were throbbing by the time I got through this line. But every medic in the line had marked my plastic dog chain card.

Feeling proud of my completed card, I wondered why no one had taken it from me to file it yet. Then I noticed another line. This line was for the blood drawing. Excellent, just what I needed was the military sucking more life out of me. I was so exhausted! As I waited anxiously in line, I heard strange noises from the blood workroom.

When my turn came, they motioned me into the room. I was appalled by what I saw. The personnel were dressed in what looked like full Hazmat gear. Biohazard suits and face shields, with the gloves and goggles and everything. They were dressed for a moon walk, not a medical procedure!

I had never seen anything like it. It all seemed so unnecessary to me. I've had blood drawn before and no one had ever donned such gear.

As others filed in around me, blood cascaded into the air from the vein of a young sailor (who looked terrified) in the back of the room. Upon seeing this geyser, one of my fellow recruits went into a fit of hysteria and fear. As he got more and more out of control, people all over the room began trying to subdue him. Eventually, they held him down on a table to draw the blood.

Grown men were crying and others were trying to convince the staff that blood did not need to be taken from them. Some had even passed out. It was a war zone! Witnessing all this chaos did not ease my mind about having blood drawn, although I was not nervous about it prior to walking into that room.

One of the young medics (in full moonwalker gear) called me to her chair. As I sat down, I mentioned to her that I had good veins and I knew they should be easy to locate without a lot of squirting. That blood geyser had been very unnerving.

I asked about her qualifications and why her colleagues seemed to be so bad at doing their job. She obviously did not find me amusing, but she said nothing. Apparently, she knew what they had in store for me next. My blood drawing commenced without incident and I didn't even cry.

I walked out of the blood workroom unharmed, more than ready to eat and believing I was finished with morning torture. I was paired up with my rack mate and sent into a back room. "Drop your pants and bend over, recruits." We hung our heads and did as we were told, side by side. At least we were allowed to endure such a humiliating and painful experience in pairs. For the grand finale, the Navy gave it to us in the rear, literally. Penicillin is evil. My newfound friend and I were sent back to our group to (what else?) wait. We ended up on the floor with 50 other recruits, rubbing our butts. The next two days were pure hell as we tried to march with our wounded fannies. Except the guy who was allergic to penicillin. That bum!

My mom always found it funny that the Marines postured to be so tough and strong, yet she was always sure to have them sit down before she uncapped a needle of any kind. She could almost guarantee that he would faint like a woman.

She joked that the government better keep this a secret or we were sure to lose any future war. All the enemy had to do, she said, was to unveil a needle in front of our Marines and fully one-third would faint dead away. America's finest, defeated by exposed needles. After my experience in the Navy, that doesn't seem so far-fetched.

There are some things that you will never know about your husband's training. There are things he chooses not to share and that he has forgotten (be it on purpose or otherwise). There are a lot of things about boot camp, training, and the military that you and I will never know. Thank God and Gov.

Although he may be tough to deal with at times, the best thing that you can do for him is to understand that sometimes, you just won't understand. Realize that he has the right to be irrational sometimes, just as much as you do.

We all have our problems, and the military tends to inflict them more than remedy them. No one will ever understand exactly what you are going through, no matter how hard they try. You will never understand exactly what your husband is going through, as much as you may think that you do.

Most of all, you can never *fully* understand each other. Accept this and stay open minded about his behavior and character flaws. Hopefully, he will do the same for you.

Q & A

Q. My husband is currently with what has got to be one of the worst command in the United States Navy . . .

A. News flash! Everyone's husband is with the worst command. It's called the government command, and that's how they operate. Sorry.

Q. My husband is an E-4 and stationed on a ship. He is called a "Petty Officer." Is he "petty" because he did not attend college, like his division officer did?

A. Well, if that is the meaning behind that, then I don't want to know why they call E-2s "Seamen!" "Petty Officer" is no more than a title.

Q. Josh's unit is not very supportive.

A. And . . . ? Whose is?

Q. My husband is cheating on me and has been for over a year. I thought the military didn't tolerate this sort of thing?

A. Yes, they don't as long as you have sufficient proof. This consists of things such as (but not limited to) his mistress's full name, age, date of birth, social security number, federal background check, high school yearbook, medical records, and a photo of him actually doing the deed with her. Don't forget to include in your pile of paperwork that the woman in the picture is, in fact, NOT his wife. They tend to miss facts like that. My advice? Just divorce him! The military only runs the morale police when it suits them.

Q. I am confused with all this school . . . what is my husband's job?

A. To practice for war and do anything else the military says.

Q. My husband says he is owned by the Army. How can anyone like that kind of life? Not only like it, but *love* it?

A. It's a wonderful thing to be controlled. Why do you think he got married?

Foreword: Army Jeeps; A Lesson in Military Philosophy

My mother worked in the emergency room as a nurse at the Tripler Army Medical Center in Hawaii. Although I was a small child at the time, I remember her being absent a lot. I would watch her put on her uniforms in the morning and thought she must be in charge of the whole hospital. I seldom heard about what went on at her workplace, and I rarely questioned it. It was not until years later that I heard this story.

Somewhere on the base, there was a car accident that the local EMS had run to the emergency room. Though there was more than one injured person, one man caught my mother's attention. A doctor was attempting to perform a very painful procedure (without anesthesia) on a hysterical young sailor. As the man flailed about, the doctor made no attempt to calm him. He just restrained his arms and legs and tried to proceed. Instead, he gave orders for him to "hold still" and "shut up" as he continued the procedure.

As my mother entered the room, she realized that this particular procedure was routinely done with the use of anesthesia in civilian hospitals because it was so painful. She suggested to the doctor that anesthesia may be the best solution to relax the man and make the procedure easier for all involved. The doctor refused. She sat there for a few moments longer as she observed the ongoing struggle.

After several minutes with no luck, the man continued to scream and carry on. At last, my mother protested bravely. "Doctor, it is obvious that this man does not want the procedure, so maybe he is best left alone?" The doctor's response left her speechless. "It doesn't matter whether he wants it or not, he is in the military. Do you ask a jeep if it wants to be worked on?"

After that, my mother always told me that if she got into a car accident, the last thing she would do before passing out would be to throw her military ID out and pray that they never found it.

CHAPTER 5

The Many Benefits That May Appall You

Ain't No Free Lunch Here!

Before we get into the benefit area, I would like to explain something that has been mistaken by many and understood by few. I am sure that you have heard the term "There is no free lunch." If this is true anywhere, it is true in the military. Rule #5: *There is nothing free in the military.* You will hear many military folks (especially recruiters) boast about the military's great "free" benefits. They try to dress up your paycheck by saying that the benefits make up for the low income.

Here is the clincher: It's not free! They secretly remove it from your paycheck before you even get it. It's almost like taxes, but sneakier, because many fail to examine their LES carefully and don't know what they are buying.

If you ever learn how to read an LES, you will notice these things. This skill will come after lots of frustration. And, like many invaluable skills obtained in the military, it is virtually useless once you get out. By the way, your husband will *never* know how to read his LES.

TRICARE: The Vicious Cycle

TRICARE, it seems, is the most loved and revered military benefit overall. Free health care! As mentioned before, it's not free. TRICARE realizes that you did not choose them as a carrier. You were simply given to them. They will never treat you as a customer, no matter how much your husband's LES says they are deducting.

As the family secretary, you will be calling TRICARE 95 percent to 100 percent of the time. So you should know that calling TRICARE is an adventure every time. If anyone in your family ever needs immediate attention, it will take you quite a while (probably longer than usual) to get through their exhaustive automated system . . . maybe years. If you have a child or any other person in the room, don't call them until you are alone.

The military, in its infinite wisdom, decided to do away with the age-old method of "pressing 1 if you are . . ." They have replaced it with a new "state-of-the-art" system that is ten times more confusing. Leave it to the Gov to mess up something that already sucked. I would rather suffer through my ailments alone than dial TRICARE's 1-800 number for the umpteenth time. It accomplishes nothing but frustration.

Their new system requires that you have a pretend conversation with a machine. When you try to follow the directions or discuss your concern, it informs you that it does not understand what you said and puts you on hold (for an hour) to talk to a person (who is sometimes less helpful than the machine).

When you finally do get someone on the line, they treat you as if *you* are the pain in the ass. It is your fault if anyone in your family needs some sort of specialty appointment. Due to other pains like yourself, there are no available appointments for the next couple of years. This will be followed by a wholehearted "sorry."

You will then be told to call back "first thing in the morning" (like you get up at that hour) to see if anyone has cancelled their appointment (which they have probably been waiting a couple years for as well). Since you can't afford a nice, easy civilian doctor yourself, you call back in the morning because it is your only choice, if you want to be seen.

You will end up staying in this same viscous TRICARE cycle until you are, in fact, forced to scream "mental health" into their automated system because you feel like going on a killing spree directed at TRICARE employees. They are the epitome of intelligence, and they represent the military quite accurately.

Remember, if you see a civilian doctor (or someone out of your area), you will be receiving medical bills from them. At least, until they can no longer keep up with your many changes of address. When you try and discuss these bills with TRICARE, they will tell you that they are missing a paper (which they lost) and that *you* need to remedy it. This will require that you complete their work and spend your time acquiring something that they will probably lose again anyway. Did I suggest earlier that you copy and file *everything*?

All in all, the TRICARE experience is in no way unique. I'm sure there are many people that have this sort of relationship with their insurance companies, so perhaps, this is not a uniquely military problem. However, us military wives find it more bothersome simply because of our husband's job, and because of that recruiter who told us how great TRICARE is. And of course, because we are so used to living in the lap of luxury.

My hope is lost for every insurance company on the planet. If TRICARE is the greatest on earth (as many contend), we are all going to die from a routine ailment while waiting for TRICARE to get around to us.

Does TRICARE Actually Cover Anything?

Eye care in the military is often a mystery. To break it down, TRICARE will cover an "eyeglass" exam. That is all. They will not cover the exam for contact lenses and they will not cover the glasses or the contacts themselves. On the positive side, contact lenses are hopefully the biggest medical expense that you will be dealing with for the next few years. TRICARE does cover dental, if you sign up for it. It will not cover any dental procedure that they consider "cosmetic." Interestingly enough, some base hospitals do offer cosmetic surgery. This includes face-lifts, boob jobs, and tummy-tucks, just to name a few.

The question of whether or not you want the military doctors doing major plastic surgery on you is yours to consider. These things will not be covered unless they are offered at the military instillation near you. There is usually a considerable waiting list (TRICARE does not advertise this very much, by the way). It seems to be a very well-kept military secret. As far as other coverages go, as long as you are going to a military hospital and you have no specialty (read: pain-in-the-ass) problems, you should be completely covered with no real concerns. Prescriptions will be free if you are getting them from the base pharmacy. If you choose a civilian pharmacy or doctor, many times there will be a small co-pay from $3-9 per month.

The great thing I have found about TRICARE as an insurance company is that they do cover birth control. Many insurance companies don't. They also cover the full cost of prenatal care and birth in their facilities, except maybe $12-15 per day that they charge after your baby is born (for the hospital bed or the food). They also cover home births.

Overall, you can receive the best or worst care in the world from military doctors, just like in the civilian world. There are many complaints about base hospitals and faculty. There are also many praises.

To help avoid someone making a mistake medically, always ask a lot of questions. If you don't like or trust your provider, ask for another. You have that right, whether you are at a military hospital or otherwise. If any provider ever makes you feel uncomfortable, report your concern and do not return under his/her care.

If you choose to go off the base for care (or the base hospital sends you off base for a specialty appointment), you will be dealing with a lot of paperwork, hassle and expense. I have found that, for convenience alone, the base hospital is the best choice.

Considering that there are mediocre and marginal doctors in any given hospital, I don't feel any more endangered in a base hospital than a civilian one. But if you are concerned about military medical care, go to a civilian and make yourself feel better. It's your life and you will be the one doing the paperwork. You should get all the facts and weigh the differences before making this choice yourself. Try the TRICARE website, since calling them is a real hassle. www.tricare.osd.mil

Mistakes: Percocet Is Almost Like Prozac (?)

There came a time when my extremely reckless husband fell off something and managed to break his arm in the process. He arrived home after work (having visited the hospital) with a cast. He seemed to be in a pissy mood and he didn't want to do anything or go anywhere.

As the night progressed, he started a ridiculous fight with me over something that I can no longer remember. After fighting vehemently for a couple hours, I finally decided to spend the night on the couch. But always unable to follow through, I waited until he was asleep and crawled back into bed with him. Hey, it was my bed too!

When he awoke in the morning, he was in the most cheery of moods. It was weird. He didn't seem to notice my silence and even had the nerve to kiss me before going to work. What the hell was his problem?

Later that day, I received a phone call from him. "What happened last night?" Interesting. So naturally, I told him he was a complete jackass. He remembered nothing. Evidentially, the Naval Hospital Pharmacy had contacted the command because they had made a mistake. They had accidentally dispensed Prozac (an antidepressant) to him, rather than Percocet (a pain medication).

Had this happened in a civilian pharmacy, there would have been mass hysteria followed by a lawsuit if the person had taken the drug with such adverse effects. I don't know how they could have been so careless. I have never known pharmacists to make a mistake like this, and I am a pharmacy tech.

My husband and I look back on that now and laugh. Well, I do at least; he doesn't remember it. However, at the time, it was extremely serious and traumatic.

Everyone is bound to make a mistake once in a while. Hospitals and medical professionals are no exception, as much as we would like to think otherwise. Always keep this in mind when dealing with any professional and be sure to examine all medication and ask questions if you are uncertain about it. Instruct your husband to do the same. No one is responsible for your safety more than yourself.

The Brown Recluse

Sometimes, military hospitals are your smallest concern. Getting to the hospital is often an adventure on its own. When your loved one presents with an illness, not all military personnel are adept enough to realize it. We have all heard the testaments of the men who received Motrin for broken legs and were similarly tortured in boot camp.

After boot camp, my husband was briefly stationed in Camp Pendelton, California, before he was permanently stationed in North Carolina. And, for the record, my husband seems to be considerably accident prone, so don't let this overly concern you.

As he slept in his tent one night during field training, there was an intruder in his sleeping bag. Already the victim of countless mosquitoes, ticks and fleas, he was dead to the world . . . He was also oblivious to the fact that there was a brown recluse taking residence in his quarters.

When he awoke one particular morning, he found that his face and jaw were throbbing. Due to the fact that he had no mirror (as he was in the field), he relied on his buddies instead. Dressing himself and emerging from his tent, he asked a group of pals if he had anything on his face. They all responded in the negative.

Through breakfast, he continued to ask if there was anything wrong with his face, since chewing his food was so painful. They continued to reassure him that he was fine, and that there was nothing wrong with either him or his face.

After morning chow, they proceeded to formation. As they assembled into smooth rows and stood at attention, the MSgt. began his morning lecture. He was interrupted when he saw my husband's face. "Holy shit, Martin, what in the hell happened to your face?" Unbeknownst to him, my husband's face was not only swollen, but also black and blue. He had a brown recluse spider bite that needed treatment. He ended up being life-flighted to the hospital because his infection was so severe. Though he got through it all right, had his friends warned him, he would have been better off.

I tell you this story to illustrate a point. That is that, the hospital does not *have* to make a mistake for something to go wrong, people can mess things up on their own. My husband had no complaints about the treatment he received at the military hospital. The only beef he still has is with the guys who didn't tell him he had an obvious problem going on.

Feres Doctrine

The Feres Doctrine. This not-so-famous piece of literature states unequivocally that there will be absolutely no legal action taken against the military by a service member. While you yourself (as a dependent) retain the right to sue the government, your husband does not. The pen truly is mightier than the sword. Your husband probably did not realize that before he used his big fat pen to sign up for boot camp. As I have said before, the military takes away most basic civil rights, and the right to representation is one of them.

This means that you must look after your poor, accident-prone husband and always encourage him to stand up for himself. Sometimes, it takes more than a couple of Motrin to heal a belly wound, and sometimes, hydration is only the first step in healing a broken bone. Remember, if they break him, he can't sue them for it. He belongs to them. Start encouraging your man!

Myths about Money

Truth #6: *The military reserves the right not to pay your husband.* They do own him, after all. It is silly to think that payment is required! It's not as if he can quit and get a new job now, is it? If they feel the need to stop paying you because, for instance, they believe they have overpaid you for the past few months (by accident), then yes, they can do that. And they will! They can also force him to pay for food and lodging while he is on deployment, leaving you with a critical shortage of pay. (They also overcharge for that food and lodging.) Don't bother wasting your time calling the officials to complain about such oversights. When it comes to money, the Gov overpays for everything, but by God, they will not overpay for something as expendable as men!

And no, they do not care if you go bankrupt, get evicted, can't pay Junior's tuition, or starve to death! That is not their problem. All they really care about is that your husband shows up in the morning to work for them. Since he will be facing federal charges if he doesn't, he cannot get another job to make more money. Nice try, though.

There are several different things that can arise as far as your pay goes, and I want to warn you of potential problems. These are not the only problems that can occur, but are the most common.

It has happened that the military "forgets" to pay you. This usually happens while the service member is switching his direct deposit from one account to another, or making a similar change. Make changes like this as seldom as possible to avoid confusing the poor dears and creating problems for yourselves.

Another possibility is that they have found an accounting mistake and they have overpaid you in the past. The military's brilliant solution to this is to suspend pay until they have gotten everything that they believe was overpaid. They feel no need to notify you of this in advance.

A man my mother knew in the Gulf War remained overseas past his ETS (End of Time in Service). The military never thought to send him home. Rather, they decided to stop his pay to his wife and children at home, leaving them without a check on payday, until the soldier could handle it from the other side of the world during the war. Yea, Army, way to go! For this reason, you would be wise to know how much money should be in your account at all times. If for any reason, there are extra funds in your account (that should not be there), the military may have overpaid you. Do not spend this extra cash or you will be paying for it in the future: it is not a gift or an interest-free loan. No, they do not have to let you return it in payments. If they do find it in the goodness of their hearts to let you pay it back in increments, they will charge interest.

The military has also been known to tell you that you have been overpaid after your husband gets out of the military. You may think that there is nothing they can do to get this money back, and that it is their fault for overpaying you—untrue. If you decide not to pay them, they will take the money out of your next federal income tax return. They can do anything they want. They are the Gov, after all.

If while monitoring your account or LES (Leave and Earning Statement), you realize that you are being *underpaid* for any reason, report it immediately. If you wait too long, they will not have to return that money to you ever. Funny how these mistakes never work out to your advantage.

During a deployment, the military can also stop paying rations. This money is currently about $200 per month and it is special money that the military gives your husband to replace his base meal card. It is supposed to be a food allowance. What no one will tell you is that while he is deployed, they have every right to take that away, leaving your family with $200/month less for groceries.

They figure that since he is eating their MREs (Meals Ready to Eat), they can charge for them, and they do not care if you and your children eat or not. It's *his* food allowance. Make sure that someone makes it clear to you before he leaves, whether or not they will be taking these funds so that you can be prepared.

I have known them to keep giving the rations pay for the entire deployment and then take them out in a lump sum when the serviceman returns home, leaving the family with the absence of an entire paycheck. Time to scramble? Yes. But it sure makes life more interesting, doesn't it?

Just as they can delay deducting funds, they can delay adding them as well. Although you are supposed to receive some sort of separation pay while your husband is stationed overseas (or if you are both living overseas—Cost of Living or COLA), they will sometimes forget this also. It's up to you to point out their oversight.

Sometimes, this can work to your advantage because you will get it all in a lump sum whenever they figure out that you were supposed to get it. But you do need to bother them about it because if they "forget" for too long, you will end up never receiving this money. Keep in mind also that if he is promoted, you may see another delay in the extra money for the promotion money reaching your account.

If you move onto base housing and they continue to give you your housing allowance, **do not spend it**. Rest assured, they will eventually realize their mistake and will take proper action to correct it. The BAH (Basic Allowance for Housing) is a considerable sum, and can add up quickly to a large debt. You will be deeply sorry if you spend that money, but the military will not care. They will take it back, sorry or not.

Like I have said, these are just a few of the most common money problems facing servicemen today. Who knows what they may do tomorrow or what the Gov will think of next? It's all about excitement in the military, no?

Your best bet is to learn how to read the LES. Understand where those moneys come from and what they are for. Be conscious that the LES matches what is going into your account and do not spend anything that you don't know for sure is yours. The military tries to prevent these mistakes, but only you can prevent them from hurting you financially.

Military Programs

There are military programs for a varying amount of projects that you can get involved in at any military base. Although I don't have a very good opinion about these things in general, I will do my best to speak positively about them.

When you arrive at your first duty station, you are supposed to be welcomed by someone who can tell you about all the fabulous things on your new base. This person is usually another wife who volunteered.

I did not receive this call until after I had been at our first duty station for a year. Many wives I know never received this call. It is, however, easy enough to find out about this program and others simply by looking them up in the phone book, checking public base facilities (bulletin boards, base paper), or asking around in the right places. Housing and transportation offices on base are particularly informative about these things.

As I don't know what all the services call their programs, I will refrain from referring to them by name. Know that they differ in minor ways between branches. There is a so-called military wife program that is supposed to inform you of your many options about these things and explain ways to save money by using the base facilities. It is not very helpful, in my experience. Many women come out of this class more confused about everything except for the TRICARE benefits. I'm sure that these classes all vary from base to base, so I would recommend trying one out just in case you hear about something that interests you.

There is usually also a program for helping military spouses to get jobs on base. In my experience, these jobs are usually throwaways and not worth the time and paperwork you have to go through to get them. You could just as easily get a minimum-wage job off-base. But there is an employment office on most bases and they are as helpful as any military organization. Individual programs vary, of course.

Every time your husband is scheduled for a deployment, there may (or may not) be a class about why your husband is going on this deployment and what is expected of you while he is gone. This seems to be another military effort to make wives feel important and ensure spousal support for the deployment. You will gain access to no real information and you will often be bored.

There are an infinite number of different programs that the military runs for pregnant women. They vary in name, but I found them insulting. These consist of classes on how to change diapers and hold a baby, all the way to what meds you are "allowed" to take during your pregnancy.

You will not have to go looking for these; you will be bombarded with them. They also have Lamaze classes, which are "required." You can decide for yourself about that class. I personally don't believe in Lamaze; I believe in epidurals.

If you are having marital discord, there is a weekend therapy trip that you can go on. I have never used this, nor have I used base chaplains or other mental care options. Personally, I like to keep my insanity private and within the family. But I have heard that the CREDO program can do wonders for a relationship on the rocks. I have heard many nice things about chaplains who can lend advice to couples in need. TRICARE does cover the cost of metal health appointments with approved (civilian) providers, if you are not inclined to a chaplain.

There is also the JAG office which, for us, has proved itself time and time again to be absolutely useless. Don't believe the television hype. Their method seems to be based solely on procrastination. Hopefully for them, your husband will be out of the service before they ever get around to doing a thing.

Base child care providers: This is a very helpful organization that certifies home day care providers on base. They will care for your children for a predetermined amount. Also, this program will use your husband's rank to calculate how much you can afford, and the government will supplement the rest.

There is usually an emergency drop-off center available and other child care options that they can fill you in on at the child development center. Many times, meals will be provided for your child at no extra cost to you. This also presents a good work-from-home opportunity, providing that you live on base (and like children). Unfortunately, these programs are often busy and hard to get into, with long lists. Anything that you find on base that is worthwhile will have a list.

Of course, there are the really helpful base benefits, like the base movie theater, where you can purchase discounted movie tickets or get free ones. The commissary and the PX which you can (sometimes) save money at and sometimes not. This also varies between bases. You should think of the base as a miniature town, bursting with possibilities. You can find almost anything you are looking for somewhere on the base. Whether it is useful or not, that is a different story.

The next time you have a problem that arises, find out if there is a military program that may be able to assist you, either for free or for a low cost. Then get to your local phone book and look up the various offices. You are almost guaranteed to find something that you could use if you look hard enough.

MAC Flights

I'm genuinely confused about these, even after reading the rules and having it explained to me over and over again. My husband works hard day in and day out to take leave maybe once a year. Upon being granted such leave to go on our wonderful vacation, we are supposed to drive to the nearest Air Force station (possibly hours away). We receive no guarantees that there will be room for us on this flight, or on any of the connecting flights. Thus, we deal with the military bureaucracy once more, which is what we are taking a vacation to get away from to begin with.

Then, we possibly get stranded somewhere, forcing us to buy a last-minute ticket on a commercial flight just so he can make it home from leave. And, depending on the cost of that ticket, we could spend more money than if we had purchased commercial seats from the start. I don't think so. Taking a MAC flight seems like borderline insanity to me.

Many find that the AMC (Air Mobility Command) or MAC (Military Aircraft) flights are a really great benefit. However, there are many inconveniences involved that no one really informs you about. "You get what you pay for." Whether you are going on vacation or PCSing, you are using "Space Available Travel." This means that not only are you last priority, but even cargo and luggage can bump you off the flight. As far as I am concerned, I am last priority with the military on a daily basis and I am not in a hurry to be treated like that on my vacation.

I would rather save my money to buy a guaranteed seat on a civilian flight, where I will be treated (at the least) like a human. Plus there are the added benefits of being served drinks, meals, and have my complaints at least heard.

If you choose to use this method of travel, for any reason, your husband must be there to make arrangements for you. Copies of leave or PCS orders are generally required. Most of the rules are difficult to understand and they vary as widely as the different bases do. As the military works, you will be put on a list based on priority. You can wait anywhere from a few hours to a few days, just to gain priority on the list. Keep in mind that these planes fly *primarily* to conduct business for the service, so they may not even be going where you need to be.

Also, none of your connecting flights will be guaranteed either, so you may get stranded somewhere in between home and where you want to be. When it is time to return home, you face the same challenges: Extra leave will *not* be granted to your husband if he is unable to return on time. His return date is not one of their priorities, although it will certainly be yours.

If you find yourself in an emergency situation, Space-A travel definitely is not for you. When faced with the death or sickness of a family member, you will want to reach your destination as soon as possible without complications. MAC flights cannot and do not provide that service. Vacations, however, are up to you. My husband and I choose to be treated as civilians as often as possible. Military life is grueling and everyone needs a break from it. I also choose to keep a car that is under warranty, because I don't like taking risks.

If you are the type who likes to walk a tightrope without a safety net, MAC flights may be just what you need. They cater to a sense of adventure and uncertainty. It is like gambling with money you don't have. Just don't be upset if something does not go your way or if you get into trouble. Whatever the reason for leaving home, I am sure that the military will make it a memorable experience. Many families find that the MAC flights work wonderfully for them and have only positive things to say about it, as I said. For more information about this service, call your nearest Air Mobility Command (or visit www.glue.umd.edu~oard/spacea/ for more details).

Be sure that you have extra cash or credit cards if you decide to travel via AMC. Always ask them if they serve meals on their flights and what the exact rules are. Most likely, they can give you information about the length of the waiting list as well. Good luck, and have fun when you get there! Heck, have fun *getting* there!

Another Oxymoron: The Elusive "Military Discount"

While engaged on a cross-country road trip, my husband and I seriously considered divorce after being stuck in the car together for many, many hours. This was bad, since at the time, we weren't even halfway there. As we were about to kill each other, we decided to stop for the night at a motel. We were in Mississippi.

We pulled off the freeway into a small town with a lot of hotels. Evidentially, this was a tourist stop of some kind and therefore, the room rates were more expensive than we had anticipated. Since we were still in the wake of September 11 and the country was at war, we figured there would be some kind of military discount. And there was . . .

The first hotel we stopped at, I walked into the lobby, where there was a lone counter with a young clerk. The lobby was quiet. I asked what the rate was for the rooms.

She responded, "Eighty dollars."

I cringed, not wanting to pay so much. "Well, do you have a military discount?" I asked.

She responded "Yes, we do."

I noticed from her tone that she was getting annoyed with my stupid questions.

"If you take the discount it will cost you 87.99."

"Are you telling me that you will charge us more because we are in the military?" I was in utter shock.

"No," she responded, "but, we . . ."

I stopped listening right then. I gave her a good piece of my mind and made a comment about her freedom being protected by my husband and others like him. I was mad. You may think that this was an isolated incident, but I guarantee you that it's not. Some places will have rather good discounts for the military, but usually only during times of war. Other than that, maybe you can save a buck or two, but it is not likely. I recommend that you become a member of Triple A. Their discounts are much higher and surrounded by less controversy and more reliability.

As far as the words "military discount" goes, this is an oxymoron. Ever since I can remember, people have been lining up to steal money from these hardworking soldiers, Marines, airmen and seamen. Don't believe me? Just go see what happens in a town when the Gov decides to build a base there. People will start moving in, building businesses, and getting rich. Interest rates get higher, promises get more plentiful, and at the end of the day, servicemen are sitting in their barracks, wondering where their money went.

People who don't know anything about it tend to look down on the military. There seems to be very little respect for the entire profession. Apparently, people think these guys are making loads of cash, getting all of these benefits, and doing nothing . . . *unless* there is a war. Us wives' trying to convince the public of this seems hopeless.

Argue with someone in Mississippi about his or her freedom at one in the morning after a hard day of driving far from home. You will soon come to learn how this country really feels about our military and the people who serve in it.

Useless, I Mean . . . Innocent Civilians

Unfortunately, our military is here to protect the rights of the same people who say they are "tired of paying military salaries." These ungrateful civilians are not only talking about things they know nothing about, but also they probably would not say that to your face. You will hear many insults directed at military families during and after your husband's career.

It is hard for most wives not to get upset about this. And I am not saying that you shouldn't. Hey, go ahead and argue with them if you want! We, as wives, may feel that the military (in general) is useless, but we know a little more about it. It is also less insulting when it comes from the back of our own minds. The fact of the matter is, sometimes, it is true. The military may be useless, some of their practices undependable, but the men in it are not.

We need leaders to command the military and not lead it through stupidity. Unfortunately, those are the very leaders who make our military look bad and piss everyone off in the process. But the high-ranking leaders are not the ones paying the price.

I have met many useless wastes of space in the military, and the sad part is that the more useless they are, the higher the rank that they have achieved. I have yet to figure out if the military makes them this way, or if they are just this way and the military encourages it. In either case, the turds float on top.

The military is underappreciated in general by two groups of people: the Gov and the civilians. When it all comes down to it, I would rather be appreciated by the Gov (since they have the control), so don't worry too much about the civilians.

As much as democracy boasts "the people rule," that just does not seem to be the case at all. And no one seems to care what the military man or wife thinks. They are usually not allowed to have an opinion.

This was illustrated beautifully in the 2000 election, when the military men in Japan were urged to vote, and then the military forgot to get their ballots to the election on time. However, wife, you are a civilian too. And you have a right to bitch as well. You also have the right to stand up in a coffee shop, restaurant, theater or mall and tell that annoying civilian where to stick it. This might actually be quite therapeutic, and even entertaining.

I Don't Know Why . . . It's Just Our Policy.

When dealing with benefits, you are dealing with the worst the military has to offer: policy. Military policy just simply never works to your advantage. Remember, the military wrote the policy, it helps *them*.

Truth #7: *The military understands the word "policy" . . . very well.* Keep in mind that this complex government organization is run by the most moronic policies ever written. I propose that the person who wrote these military policies should be shot . . . all according to policy, of course.

If you don't know the policy on a specific thing, there is really no need to ask. No one knows the policy except for (possibly) the base commander, who has the big book as a reference . . . or the JAG. Rather than asking, I have found that it is helpful to think of the most absurd rule that has ever been thought up and then multiply its ridiculousness by three. The accuracy of this method is well documented; ask any wife. This military truth can be summed up in one quote: "It doesn't make sense, it's just our policy."

Q & A

Q. I am so frustrated with the complete lack of organization in the Army. It is completely undependable!

A. But the Army is run by the leaders of our great country! Scary, eh?

Q. I just got an angry call from the command because they "didn't know" my father-in-law just died. All the lower-ranking guys knew!

A. Gives new meaning to the words "military intelligence," doesn't it?

Q. The medical department of the Marine Corps is a thorn in my left side.

A. I agree. But I believe that the medical department of the Marine Corps is the Navy (for the record).

Q. My husband had me change the other day before we went to the commissary. I was wearing a sleeveless shirt and he said I am not allowed to wear those, or tank tops, in places like the exchange or commissary. Is it possible that he is correct?

A. Yes, it is possible that he is correct. As a matter of fact, he is correct. They do have a dress code policy. Although it is seldom enforced, the military still thinks it can boss spouses around as much as a serviceman.

Q. I think we are supposed to be getting more money than we are actually getting. When I take the earnings on his LES and subtract how much we really get, my calculations show that we are missing $170.

A. It doesn't always add up, but it can somehow be explained away by the geeks over in finance. They don't make mistakes over there, in case you were wondering.

Q. It just seems crazy to me that my husband can be punished or get into trouble for refusing to take such a dangerous medication (Malaria pill).

A. Does the military do anything that does **not** seem crazy to you? It's not a big shock if you consider the source.

Foreword: Meals Ready to Evacuate (MRE)

Pregnancy is a challenge. Pregnancy in the military is torture. I was seven months pregnant with my first child when they told my husband, a Lance Corporal in the Marine Corps, that he would be going on a one-month deployment.

Inasmuch as he was going to be living in government quarters and eating military food, they decided to also charge him for these privileges during the deployment. Since money was tight anyway, this was a large financial hardship. We only had enough money to pay for the bare necessities (less food).

Food was very important to me during my pregnancy. The week before his scheduled deployment was the week before payday. I scoured my kitchen in search of anything acceptable to eat. I was still having morning sickness, and nothing seemed appetizing. I passed on the "Rice-a-Roni" and catsup. But that's literally all we had in our kitchen. All but the packets of food that all military families know, MREs (Meals Ready to Eat).

I whined to my husband that we had no food and no money. I was starving. Although I have tasted many things in my life, I had never had an MRE. After hearing horror stories about them for my entire life, I didn't even want to try one. When my husband suggested it, I grimaced. But it was my only option after I realized we had no butter to cook the "Rice-a-Roni." Besides, how bad could it be? After all, I *was* starving!

I think it is important that I explain that MREs are not like TV dinners. They come in a squeeze-able packet. The food in them looks like it has already been digested. As I sat there in my kitchen with my spoon, looking at the nasty contents, I remembered that we would be paying for a month's worth of these while my husband was on deployment. Leave it to the military to charge us for slop.

I took only one bite before my stomach forced an evacuation. Now, I was even hungrier because I had an empty stomach. I opened packet after packet, still searching for something remotely edible, while my husband retreated to our bedroom. I threw them away one by one (after first tasting them) and rejected them all. Blah.

After I had opened a significant number of these packets (finding all of them completely unacceptable), I gave up on my quest and decided that I had lost my appetite. When I went to discard the remainder of the final opened MRE, my husband emerged: "Wait, don't throw that away! I'll eat it!"

Lesson Learned: The military can train a man to eat anything after days of starvation. However, they cannot satisfy a starving pregnant woman. Nature is not trainable, but your husband *is*.

CHAPTER 6

Subculture—The Nature of the Beast

It's Not about You, Ever

In order to understand the military, you must first understand the government. In this country, majority rules. I think that not only is the government not looking out for the best interest of this country or the majority, they are not even looking out for the best interests of the minority. By minority, I mean the lowest of all low-class citizens: the U.S. military.

The men in the military enjoy no civil rights, and they have even fewer privileges. The military will keep your husband from family holidays, vacations, surgeries, funerals, and even births. Why do they do this? It is evidently their belief that it's in the best interest of the country for your husband to be out in training at the expense of his family life.

Civil liberties must be forfeited. When your husband signs away his own rights to these things, understand that he is also signing away yours. The military will definitely teach you why the constitution is necessary.

While many times it seems unforgivable for the military not to excuse its people for the important events, you must understand that if every wife had her way, no active duty man would ever be anywhere except at home. Yes, it is unfair. But that's the way the ball rolls.

As hard as it seems, this has been happening to everyone in this country forever. It seems that no one I have met believes that they are getting a fair shake. While the Gov is inherently corrupt, it does sometimes offer a benefit that you will be grateful to have. That's why it is important to be patient. *Very patient.*

Is it best for your family if your husband misses his father's funeral because he is at war? No, it's not. Is it best for the country if your husband misses the funeral to protect or save the rights of others? The government thinks so, and so do most civilians. Your opinion and the opinions of others in the military culture has no bearing. It is very difficult to see this kind of logic . . . especially when your husband is not at war, he is just in field training!

Try to keep in mind that the military mindset is that everything they do is exceptionally important—even though, to you, it's mostly not. The bureaucratic military is a group of self-important people who are busy playing war games. Although your husband may have no interest in these games, he is a pawn taking part in them. Training for war is, after all, what he signed up to do.

Personally, I believe that most men (especially the type who joins the military) totally enjoy playing war. It is recreation for those burdened with testosterone, and incomprehensible to most women. Watch your male children, they play war games without encouragement. Nonetheless, you are immersed in a rich subculture known as the military, but run by the government. Remember that the same government runs the IRS. Things aren't always going to be rational or reasonable.

Truth #8: *If you think the military gave you a good deal, you've still got your surprise coming.* As we have previously discussed, the military organization thrives on paperwork and contracts. If you are yet to have a military wake-up call, or believe that you are an exception for any reason, you may look forward to all the wonders of the complete military experience.

Any serious promises that the military has made to you must be put in writing to be worth anything. If it is not on paper, don't expect it to happen. However, in contracts, they often include clauses that essentially say "We don't have to do anything that we have promised here." Remember that anyone writing a contract is going to write it in their best interests—not yours. The military is absolutely no exception.

That is why it is important to read entire contracts before signing them. If you are reading this, it is probably too late to do anything about the contract that got you in. However, even if your contract is golden, the military will still throw you some curve balls. Inevitably, at least one of them will smack you right in the face sooner or later.

Having a Pet

Having pets can be a complicated thing in the military. Not only do you have to worry about pet deposits at any new duty station, you also have to consider moving them, and the money that is required to accomplish it.

Many people in the military adopt pets, only to return them later because they are moving and are unable to take the animal with them. The less responsible people dump the pet before moving, leaving it to fend for itself. Ultimately, it is euthanized or dies in the elements. For this reason, there are a lot of strays that end up alone in military towns when no one else will take them.

If you already own a pet that you cannot consider leaving behind, good luck. If not, I would recommend keeping it that way. The military cannot only send you across the country, but across the world. If you receive orders to Hawaii or Japan, the question of moving your pet becomes even more challenging and costly.

The pet will have to be put in quarantine overseas for varying time periods. While they are in these quarantines, you have little control over the conditions that they are living in. A dog may get an hour to play each day and spend the rest of his time in a small cage. This could go on for months during a quarantine. Would you want to be isolated from your family for 2-3 months? How do you tell a dog that you have not abandoned him?

Of course, if you are willing and able to spend money, you have more options. The fact of the matter is, in any case, your pet will be alone, isolated and underprivileged. That will be depressing for both you and your pet.

Overall, pets represent a huge challenge during a PCS. Consequently, in military life, they also represent more paperwork. If you want to create more problems for yourself during a move, a pet is the best way to accomplish that.

You may need to take them to the vet and get prescriptions for them to sleep on a cross-country road trip or airplane ride. Your animal will probably survive quarantine if necessary, but the question of putting them through that will remain your choice. Some animals are never the same after their moving experience. You might consider having a "second home" for the animal with your parents or good friends. Then, in case you get sent overseas, you can leave them and collect them when you return from your tour. Is it a good idea to take that hairy Husky to Guam, or one of those bald cats to Alaska?

A strong argument I have for not getting a pet is that I don't want to take care of it. I am busy enough taking care of myself and my family and I have enough paperwork. No matter how badly your husband wants that German Shepherd, is he around enough to care for the dog properly? Who will be cleaning up the poop, feeding the dog, and walking it while your husband is at work? How about if he gets deployed? I'm willing to bet that this responsibility will be yours. So, your husband's dog will become your dog. Are you wanting to take it on? If you don't have a pet, don't get one unless you can move them anywhere with a clear conscience and have the financing to do so responsibly. You always have to consider moving a likely possibility as long as you remain in the military.

If you do have a pet, do not abandon them when you move. There are resources in most military towns for getting rid of an unwanted animal. This is another personal choice that only you can decide about, but please think about the consequences to your beloved Fido before rushing into anything or making impulse decision to adopt.

If you have ever crossed paths with a stray animal, you will know you need to think this over carefully. My husband and I took in a stray cat that couldn't seem to properly utilize a litter box. We decided that she was not cut out to be an inside cat. When we moved her outside, she ran away.

She came around about a year later, terribly skinny and missing an eye. I felt terrible, but was never able to take her in because she was so used to being a stray. It was a horribly sad thing and I felt completely guilty for not spending more time trying to train her. Imagine what happens to your pet when you abandon him. Then, decide if you can live with yourself after you have done such a thing.

The Military: Your New Family

Almost everyone in the military is away from their extended family. When I was a child, I did not realize that most kids visit grandma every weekend instead of every few years. Upon arriving at my first duty station as an adult, I quickly began building my own network. I created friends from strangers in a matter of months. Not long after we arrived, I had a close-knit group of friends who were willing to listen to every foolish thing I had to say, no matter what time of day I felt like saying it.

We got each other through many hard times. I seem to have created this environment for myself everywhere I have been since I became an adult. If I don't have family close by, I make one of my own. I think this is a very important aspect of surviving happily in military life, especially if you plan to do it for many years.

Since this came so naturally to me, I was shocked to discover that others my own age, even my close friends, did not feel the same way. Biology is the only family they have. I think it is a sad way to live if you are constantly away from your biological family.

If you are on or near a base, there will be many women who would like to have a friend. Most of the women married to men in the military are struggling with the same challenges that you have. They deal with the same issues, they are about the same age, and they are having (or have had) the same feelings. If you can go through these things together, you will build some fabulous friendships, as well as feel better yourself. And at the end, when it is time to leave the base, you will feel like you are leaving members of your family because you have been through so much together.

You can either mourn the distance between yourself and your family, or you can be happy that you are with your husband and build your own support group from there. Those are your choices. As I have stressed, it is your job to find support—no one will do it for you.

It's not hard to find friends if you are looking for them. In fact, one great perk relating to the military is that you have "family" everywhere.

You do not simply belong where you are born, you belong anywhere someone will take you in. Who knows, your next PCS could turn out to be a visit with someone you haven't seen since you were stationed in Hawaii! You can also save money on hotel bills this way. Someday, knowing someone in Denver could be a huge advantage for you!

Happy Holidays

Holidays in the military may come as a surprise to you, especially if you are marrying a man who has been living a single life in the military for a while. Your husband's heart may go out to all of those men who are celebrating Christmas in their barracks, his other family.

Although you may feel reluctant to let your home be open to strangers, you will be expected to for at least one significant holiday . . . by your husband. I have personally never minded this. I enjoy it. If you have no blood relatives in the vicinity to spend your holiday with, there is no reason to be inhospitable. Since few men in the military are near their family, you should feel fortunate that you and your husband have each other. Many single men in the military have no one and nowhere to go during the holidays.

One particular Thanksgiving, it was my idea to open our home. I bought the biggest turkey I could find and divvied up the cooking responsibilities with two other wives. The festivities were to take place at my house. The day before Thanksgiving, I received an angry phone call from one of the other wives. She had heard (through the grapevine) that there would be single Marines joining in our celebration and she was angry because they were not contributing food. I thought it was an incredibly awful attitude, especially since we had more than enough to go around. I ended up promising that I would have the men bring extra desserts. Although she was still unhappy, she accepted that. Regardless, we had a wonderful Thanksgiving (with more than enough food to go around) and the single Marines added much to the party.

The same wife was alone the next Thanksgiving because her husband was overseas. At 5 P.M. on Thanksgiving Day, her doorbell rang and there was one of those single Marines standing at her doorstep. He was in full gear with cammie paint, having just been released from the field after a two-week operation. Without showering or even changing, he had visited the store and rushed to her home. In his arms, he held a small Thanksgiving feast. He had visited knowing that she was depressed to be alone during the holiday and wanting to help her. He more than repaid for the hospitality she had given him (albeit unwillingly) the previous year.

Another Thanksgiving I spent on the base eating a turkey dinner in the cafeteria with the guys. These holidays and many others may not be traditional, but they will become the norm (most years) for any military family. It is almost impossible for you to go home for every holiday. Like I said, in the military, you create family out of friends—this is how you do it.

Although many of your holidays will be spent with different people over the years, you will always find yourself among friends if you choose. When you get out of the military, you may miss seeing the true holiday spirit in yourself and others. Hopefully, you will realize that the military brought you much happiness simply by throwing your husband together with a bunch of guys he never knew he would love. (Just remember that sentiment when you have 5 or 6 drunken men sleeping in your living room for the rest of the weekend.)

LOCATION, LOCATION, LOCATION

Truth #9: *You will not be "seeing the world."* Well, at least you won't be seeing the parts of the world that you always dreamed of seeing. The Gov will, however, woo you with their ability to send you to the places you never dreamed of (or wanted to be). They sent us to North Carolina. I never had any real desire to go there. If I had, I could have driven there . . . and then had the freedom of going home *without* spending a four-year enlistment there. The military is not an all-expenses-paid vacation. Even the most beautiful places in the world are not always fun places to live. In Hawaii, you must worry about tidal waves and typhoons and tropical insects. North Carolina has deadly humidity, and sunburns can occur after only 20 minutes in the sun. But there are downfalls to living anywhere. You will become jealous of others. Their duty stations will be where you have always dreamed of going, yet they will profess to be miserable there. Just know that every military base anywhere in the world is occupied by thousands of personnel who hate the place. That's how it will always be. Evidentially, the Gov believes keeping people in misery makes them more loyal.

Location, it seems, turns out to be a very big issue in the military. No one seems to think about it a lot going in. Once they get there, all of a sudden, they have a lot to say about it. Many of them long to go back to stations in their past, although they hated them while they were there. Even when the duty station you end up with is what you requested, it is still somehow less than what you expected.

I once met a girl who fell madly in love with a sailor before she realized that marrying him would take her away from everyone and everything she had ever known. I remember her comment, "It just never occurred to me that there were no naval bases in Kentucky." It seemed humorous to me at the time because even if there had been a naval base there, he probably wouldn't have been stationed at it.

I have met people who are terribly jealous of my current duty station and it just seems so crazy to me that anyone would live in North Carolina on purpose. I thought it interesting that no one liked the bases they were on, and for my own amusement, I conducted a small and very informal poll on the Internet about the most and least favorite bases in the world. I have listed my results here.

The percentages refer to the numbers of people in my poll who liked the post listed. All of those who participated in the poll had been stationed at the base in question. Those places with a zero-percent listing were from those people who said that they hated the place and would rather amputate an arm than return there. These numbers are shocking to me, and I am sure that they will be for you as well.

Marine Corps
Cherry Point, NC: 100%
Camp LeJeune 66%
Kaneohe Bay, Hawaii: 50%
Camp Pendelton: 40%
MCAS Beaufort: 0%
Yuma, AZ: 0%

Army
Ft. Shafter, HA: 100%
Ft. Bragg: 100%
Ft. Sam Houston: 66%
Ft. Hood: 50%
Ft. Lewis: 0%
Ft. Knox: 0%
Ft. Riley: 0%

Navy
San Diego, CA: 100%
Key West, FL: 100%
Norfolk, VA: 33%
Everett, Washington: 0%

Air Force
Kesler AFB: 100%
Pease AFB: 100%
Shepherd AFB: 0%

The purpose of this poll is to illustrate a point. No one really likes his or her duty stations. Most of the people polled chose a previous base as their favorite. Odds are that they hated them while they were there—And almost no one said that they liked their current base! Another interesting point, I would personally sever my own arm before going back to Camp LeJeune or Ft. Hood. However, LeJeune was met with a 100 percent approval rate and Ft. Hood, a whopping 50 percent (pretty good, if you have ever seen Ft. Hood). Conversely, my husband and I groveled at the military's feet trying to get transferred to Ft. Lewis, met in my poll with a 0% approval rating.

So as you go to your first duty station, love it or hate it, but remember, your next one could be worse!

If you have not yet reached your first duty station, please completely disregard the opinions of others listed in this poll. You are free to make your own assessment of your new home, and you will have plenty of time to do so. If you like living in Ft. Knox or Shepherd AFB, throw yourself a party because you're lucky! If you can enjoy these places, you have truly learned to grow where you have been planted.

Keep in mind that you are in for the experience of a lifetime if you move to a place that you happen to hate. You will learn things about people and yourself that you never knew. Never feel bad about knocking your duty station. So many people have been upset with me for hating North Carolina, while they completely hang my home state out to dry. People like different things and different places. I would hate to think how many people would move to the "best" place if everyone thought the same way. It is not your fault if you find sweet tea particularly nasty and you hate grits. It's not anyone else's fault that they hate the rain in the Pacific Northwest, or the lack of humidity in the desert. Find beauty where you are. From there on, it's all about your experience. Create whatever you want where you are.

Spring-Cleaning: Military Style

Most people move in to their homes over time. As this occurs, the need for "spring-cleaning" arises in a typical home. Growing up in a military family and now being responsible for my own household, I have embraced "spring-cleaning" as one of my favorite military exemptions.

After living in your home for about a year, you too will notice that your home is in need of some "organization." The drawers will be full, the closets will be packed—and you will find yourself unable to find just about anything. Fortunately, since you are a military wife now, you don't have to worry about spring-cleaning!

If a PCS is in your near future, or even a deployment, you have the option of moving. Granted, moving is not fun. No more than spring-cleaning, anyway. I find movement more exciting. Not only will you get the organization you are hoping for, you will also get a whole new environment to go with it!

I see that the military has affected me a lot in this particular area. In order to clean a bookshelf, I would completely remove the contents of it, making an even bigger mess. Then I would find a new place for everything. It is things like that which have stayed with me. A trademark of a military upbringing, if you will. Also, if you take issue with your location to begin with, the best thing about any military base is that you can bet you will not be there very long. Make your house your home, grow into it, live in it, and then get ready to vacate for spring-cleaning.

Buying American

I love cars. I always pay attention to cars. So naturally, buying a car is a big affair for me. I see them not as mere transportation, but as a statement. I have met many military couples who refuse to buy a car unless it is American made. One woman went so far as to buy a Ford Focus rather than get a car which she liked. All in the name of supporting America.

Pardon me for saying so, but we are military families . . . we *are* supporting America! That's what we do. I think your husband is sacrificing enough on behalf of America, don't you? Besides that, I don't see much of America supporting us. If Ford wanted to support us, they would offer a military discount. But since they don't, it's a fair market, and it should be for foreign-made cars as well.

It is decidedly un-American to buy a car simply because it is American. The very principal of capitalism is built on supply and demand. Everyone wants to make money, but *supposedly*, only those with the best product make money. Now, Americans are very good at a lot of things, but making cars is not one of them. So my question is, why is it that American car companies continue to make money despite the fact that their product is expensive and not built to last? Because people "buy American," that's why. When in fact, not buying American would damage the companies financially, forcing them to improve the quality and price of their vehicles. This would allow you to purchase quality American vehicles in the future.

My point is, buying a car for such a sentimental reason is absolutely ridiculous. You will continue to make payments on that Ford Focus long after your sentimental feelings wear off. Ford will get that money and move on, continuing to sell future lemons to other Americans like you. You don't make a lot of money. You cannot afford to throw it around on something that you may decide that you don't like. You need something you will keep around for a while, and that is reliable. Trust me, Ford makes enough money so your sale won't mean a lot to them. But it will mean a lot to you, so be careful.

There are good reasons to buy Fords. To support America is not one of them. If you want that Ford Focus because it's the only car you have ever wanted, then go for it. If you just think the salesman is cute and want to make his day, go right ahead. But if the sole reason you have for purchasing a car is because it is American made, I think that's a cop-out.

Consider what you want before going out to buy a vehicle. This includes price, model and size. Having a clear picture of what you want, need, and can afford will narrow it down considerably. If you are buying a used vehicle, be sure to have it examined by a mechanic (or by your husband, if he is mechanically inclined).

Remember, it would be best for you to shop around. If you live in a primarily military town, it is best to go elsewhere for a better deal. Most of all, make sure that you can enjoy your car. It will be around for a long time. By the way, if your husband is an E-1 and you don't have a job, it is not the best idea to buy a Cadillac Escalade. So don't get carried away unless you want to *live* in your car!

Small Victories: License Plates

When I was a child, I remember playing the "license plate game." The object of the game was to spot the out-of-state plates on a long road trip. We had many road trips while I was growing up, due to the military, of course. License-plate "looking" stuck with me well into my adulthood. To arrive at my husband's duty station, I drove from Washington state to North Carolina, an exhausting cross-country road trip. There also were not too many interesting landmarks along the way; it seems I have seen them all before. When I arrived in Camp LeJeune, I immediately began looking at the surrounding license plates. I had been upset about my husband's duty station because it was so far from both of our homes on the West Coast.

I have only seen one other Washington license plate in Camp LeJeune. I have met a few people from Washington, but their cars donned North Carolina plates. As it was, our license plate became a symbol of pride for us. We showed everyone that we were not from this godforsaken place; we were Washingtonians, dammit!

Although this is not normally a symbol of pride, others in the military understand. On the way home from the post office one day, we were passed by a truck with Washington plates. The driver honked and waved and gave us a thumbs up, showing us with his driver's license that he, too, was from our home state. You, too, will understand what I mean when you buy a new car at your first duty station. And as you request the registration from your husband's home of record, you will feel the same relief and pride that we felt for our Washington plates because you are, at least, able to attain some proof that you are from somewhere other than *here*.

Age-Old Wars: Officers vs. Enlisted

If your husband is enlisted, this may become a really important issue in your household (or it may not). Enlisted folks seem to wrestle with a professional inferiority complex a lot. The fact is that officers get paid more because they went to college. They are doing a job just like your husband is, and no one is better or worse off for it.

Being the daughter of an officer and the wife of an enlisted man, I have noticed the differences between each type of household. The officers are just as underpaid and underappreciated. Do *you* want to spend 8 years studying in college only to make $100k less than you are worth? The officers (in my opinion) are much smarter about this because they don't seem to put any of their energy into hating the enlisted men. Enlisted men often spend time feeling inferior and dissing officers for making more money.

What the hell is wrong with making more money? I thought everyone's goal in life was to make more and do less. Why hate someone for that? People who don't work for their money are my heroes and role models. I wish I was a famous actress so that I could accomplish as much!

On a side note, most officers (especially with a medical specialty) work longer and harder for their money than any enlisted man ever dreamed. The new private is just as clueless as the new lieutenant. One is just getting paid a little more, but not much. So here is a little tip: If you don't worry about the officers, they won't worry about you. Sometimes, you will run into a wife who feels that, since her husband has considerable (officers) rank, she should be respected more. You run into these women just as often in the enlisted world. They are the crusty old (bitter) wives!

There is no use in feeling jealous of other wives because they make more money. Spouses of lower-ranking officers are crapped all over and snubbed as much as any enlisted spouse ever was. The really big advantage of enlistment is that a high-ranking enlisted man is revered by the military and by officers. High-ranking officers often struggle for the respect of the enlisted crowd while still being paid pennies on the dollar to do their jobs.

As in all walks of life, you can't judge a book by its cover, or in this case, a man by his collar. People get very touchy about this subject. Bringing it up will anger people and cause them to become defensive. It's kind of like bringing up the topic of abortion. Now that you know this, I will leave you to decide whether it is a worthy topic for discussion or if you would rather not waste your time worrying about things that just don't matter.

September 11

September 11 is a day that will live in infamy throughout the country, if not the world, much like Pearl Harbor was, a generation before us. In the generations to come, there will likely be more attempts made to demolish the spirit of our country. As I write this, it has been almost a full year since the attacks on the World Trade Center and the Pentagon. Yet the Pentagon attack has been almost completely submerged. On Memorial Day (a day to honor the military and veterans), I heard a tribute that said the Memorial Day celebration was dedicated to "those who gave all in service, AND the victims of the attacks." When did these people volunteer to dedicate their lives to our country? Last I checked, they were just going to work that day, like all the rest of the civilians. The people who did volunteer were the police and firemen, and I am certain that many police and firemen have lost their lives since that day.

I feel very bad for the victims and their families. I cannot imagine losing a loved one in that way. However, I can imagine my husband being sent to the edge of the world to fight the very people who attacked us that day in their environment. Which, by the way, he is doing (with the help of countless other Marines, seamen, soldiers, and airmen). Where are their tributes? When will Whitney Houston sing for them? The victims of September 11 have been martyred long enough. It is time to turn the attention to the real forgotten heroes who are fighting for our country today, and every day (during war *and* peace). The attack did not kill our spirit, but revealed it. Maybe we should thank Osama.

As I see it, September 11 was a mixed blessing for our military. Sure, we have to fight another war, but at least now, we are getting some recognition. (Not to mention that the civilians aren't protesting our puny raises *as* often.) No one had thought about the military since the Gulf War, until September 11. How many flags were flying before that day? And all because civilians lost their lives. Military personnel are losing their lives every day, leaving widows and children, whom no one thinks twice about. It makes me sad to think that my husband's life is worth less somehow, just because he does not go to work in the Trade Center. The point is that civilians had all but forgotten about the military until they decided that they *needed* them.

Shortly after September 11, there were men on the radio screaming that if there was a draft, they would not go. Their lives were too "important" and they were too "busy" to fight for freedom. But they were still "all for the war, as long as they didn't have to go." Besides, that's why we have a military, right? So volunteers with nothing better to do can die instead. It doesn't surprise me that other countries call Americans vain and selfish, look who we put on the radio!

This has been the hardest thing for me to accept about military life. Not that I have to say goodbye once in a while, not to give up my sense of security and control so that Americans can have it instead, but to learn that Americans just really don't *care*. I guess we are all going to have to get used to being taken for granted, until the people of this country wake up and realize that the military is here to protect them, and start being a little more grateful about it.

Fraternization

Like the September 11 issue and like the officer topic, this is also a very sensitive subject. Fraternization is a big issue in the military because it can ruin careers . . . period. Pvt. Johnson is a friend of Col. McDonald. No problem, right? Fast-forward to a wartime situation. Col. McDonald has to send one man on a mission that he knows is very risky or even deadly. He has to chose between Pvt. Johnson (his friend) and your husband (who is not his friend) and knowingly send one of them to his death. Who do you think he will choose? Now that is a big problem! Right? That is the reason that fraternization is not allowed, not because the military hates anyone, but because it is unfair to others if one person has an advantage like that over another. I am sure you don't like it in any situation when others are favored over you. If you don't want your husband to get in trouble, follow the rules. It does not matter if you don't like the rules; all that matters is that you follow them. Is it more important for your husband to keep his rank, or for you to be allowed to hang out with an officer?

The Rattlesnake

During a field op, my husband came across one of his buddies sleeping. Upon closer inspection, he noticed that his friend had a large rattlesnake curled up on his chest. He now faced a dilemma. If he woke the sleeping man, he may get startled or panic, causing the rattlesnake to bite him. Since they were in the field, the bitten buddy may not get the snake antivenom in a timely fashion. He chose to remove the snake from his sleeping friend himself. He used the butt of his rifle to perform a "golf club removal maneuver" on the snake. In doing so, he gave the snake a good whack, hurling it across the camp, where it met an untimely death at the hands of another Marine standing by with a shovel.

In my opinion, he adapted to and overcame the unfortunate

situation. This is precisely the type of thing that the military encourages . . . or so I thought.

When the command heard rumor about the daring rescue operation, they immediately wrote him up. Unbeknownst to us, rattlesnakes at that time and place (some wildlife refuge?) were a protected species, and not allowed to be killed under federal laws. The command wrote him up on charges and threatened to fine him and demote him. I thought he deserved a medal.

This brings me to truth #10: *Someone is always to blame in the military.* Remember this when the calls start coming in at 3 in the morning because one of your husband's men was unfairly imprisoned, *again.* Someone is responsible for his actions other than himself, and this person could be your husband. Accidents happen sometimes though, right? Wrong. If there is an accident, there will be an investigation and someone will lose his career. I once saw an officer blamed for an accident (resulting in a death) that he was not even present in. He was promptly kicked out of the military, losing all benefits and with a lasting stigma. The military does not do this to be unfair; they do it for the same reason your children point at each other when something gets broken. The military, much like having children, is a full-time job that stays with you. I have not yet decided which is more trying.

The Military Is Not Fair

Something you need to always be aware of is that the military classifies everything. No matter what you are trying to get from them, you will be put on a priority-based list. This ranges from housing to medical treatment. If you realize this and accept it, your life will be made easier. No one gets to start at the top of the list for everything. But in time, they will get to you. Maybe.

So many feel that the military should cater to *her* every need. She may be filled with anger based on misinformation, or feels that the military owes her something. Wake-up call: The military owes you nothing. They are not here to please you and they have no obligation to do things in a timely fashion. The military will never do anything just to make you happy. The sooner you get used to the fact that the military is not fair, the happier you will be.

Too many wives are shooting the messenger, so to speak. It reflects poorly on them, as well as on their husbands. The military has treated countless people just as unfairly as you. Some more unfairly.

If you find your situation particularly horrible, just ask around and you will almost certainly find that other wives have endured similar or worse injustices. It doesn't matter how much you have suffered, there is always someone who has suffered more. There is no reason to be disrespected by the military, but there is also no reason to disrespect others because of the military. Cheerful people often find that they make others feel good too. Although yourself and your family are number one to *you*, they are not to the military. That's why you are there. You represent your family and their needs. You are the advocate. *You* fight for what is best for your family. If you do nothing but bitch, moan, and complain, your family will not be benefitting from you *or* the military. Certainly, nothing will be handed to you. There is a huge difference between standing up for yourself to get what you need and yelling at people to get what you want.

If you find that you are one of these uncontrollable wives who tends to fly off at the handle, don't be surprised if someone corrects your inappropriate behavior. There is little sympathy for complaints, especially among senior wives. Making fun of your situation is appropriate; complaining about it is tolerated only for a short time. It won't be long before your fellow wives, your husband's command, and even your parents grow tired and unconcerned with your personal sense of injustice. Someone is likely to tell you so. There is a time for complaints and a time to overcome. If you are wise, you will practice overcoming frequently in the years ahead. Remember, you chose the military, it did not choose you. You are now to abide by their rules, as you have agreed to do. You cannot change it, you cannot fix it and you cannot make one of the military's own see it your way. Sorry, tough break. I have dealt with it, your neighbor has dealt with it, your husband has to deal with it, and you need to deal with it, too. Life is not fair and neither is the military!

Q & A

Q. I am so tired of buying military things. His things keep "disappearing" over and over!

A. Sounds like your husband needs to pay more attention to his things. The military has no way to filter out thievery; it needs to be prevented with personal awareness about one's expensive gear. People *do* steal in the military.

Q. My parents want us to wait before we get married, but we cannot afford to live on his salary. I want to get married at the Justice of the Peace, but I know my parents will not approve. They want a big wedding. What should I do?

A. Do your parents have to live on your budget? Are you an adult? Make your own choices and do what is best for you.

Q. My husband told me that any other position besides "missionary" is against the law in the military. He also told me that oral sex was not allowed. Is this true or was he kidding?

A. No, he was not kidding, and yes, it is true. They can use the UCMJ under the "sodomy" infringement and court-martial him. Be thankful that they allow either of you to have sex at all. Translation: Don't get caught. It is an unenforceable rule, as long as you are not being outwardly blatant.

Q. We pay for our base housing and there isn't even a fridge or dishwasher furnished!

A. I pay for my apartment and neither are provided either. What's your point? Move off-base if you don't like the facilities. You do have a choice.

Q. My husband won a promotion board, but now he has to wait in line to be promoted . . . why?

A. The military makes a line out of anything. But they do have a quota. There can only be a certain number of any given rank at any given time. He has to wait for a spot to open. They do this so that they don't get too many chiefs and not enough Indians. After all, the Indians are important too.

CHAPTER 7

Moving (and Moving Again . . . and Again)

Moving As a Way of Life

There are some people in this world that, no matter how hard they try, they cannot seem to handle moving. Since I have been dealing with it my whole life, I never understood how a woman could possibly marry into the military and not expect to be moved around.

One day, I was watching a movie about Alaska. People living in Alaska deal with a massive amount of snow on a daily basis most of the year. This is not just shoveling the driveway once in a while; I'm talking layers upon layers of snow and ice.

All of this snow and ice seems so foreign to me . . . I considered these people weird and I wondered how they dealt with it. I gradually realized that they were just like me. Sure, they know that people live in places where snow does not fall, but they don't mind their way of life because they have never known anything different. Just like I know that some people stay in their hometown and never leave. I guess Alaskans may even believe that people from warm climates like Texas and California are the weird ones!

If I were moving to Alaska, I'm sure I would be in for some surprises. Snow is a way of life for these people. Although I know what snow is, I don't know what it's like to deal with it all the time, just as many new wives don't know how to deal with moving as a way of life, or even the military as a way of life, for that matter. I could offer many examples of the above story. People in Washington deal with rain all their lives, people in the tropics deal with humidity all their lives, and military wives deal with anything the military hands us all our lives (be it rain, humidity, snow or changing duty stations).

Not everyone is cut out for this, just as I am not cut out to live in Alaska. But maybe I am, I have just never tried it. Humans are very adaptable creatures. (Hopefully, Uncle Sam is not reading, or I will certainly end up in Alaska *now*.) Anyone can deal with the military for a short period of their lives, mainly because they have to. There is no going back. Once you are in, you endure or you die. Just like in Alaska—you wear the coat or you freeze to death. It's up to you what you want to do, but keep in mind that it is up to you to make the best of your snowy days. The military isn't so bad and it is definitely not worth being unhappy over. Believe me, I know from experience. Life is too short, enjoy that snow!

Orders at Last . . . to WHERE?!!

So you have orders. You finally know where you are going! After all that schooling and boot camp and separation, you will finally be settled! I'm sure you are very excited about living in . . . Ft. Knox. Try not to be too overwhelmed with joy. Kind of anti-climactic, eh?

This brings us to the revered truth #11: *You will never "pick" your duty station.* Your husband has relinquished control of his body and soul to the military and no one else. If you choose to join him on his journey to hell, you can expect just that—an all-expenses-paid trip to your version of hell. When your husband joins the military, they will give him a piece of paper (commonly referred to as the "wish list") and tell him to write down his first choice of post. One will assume that this means they are doing everything in their power to get you there, right? Umm, no.

No one knows for sure the *real* reason for the wish list. Tradition, perhaps? Torture? Maybe. I believe it is for data-entry purposes. This way, while they are deciding where to send him, they can look it up. Then, they can take out a ruler and measure on the map 12 inches (or halfway around the world) from where you want to be. This is where they will send you. I can imagine the glee of the employees in this secret personnel office. In truth, the wish list is the military's lame attempt to give you the illusion of control. In reality, you have no control. If you think you have control, it is an illusion. Now that we have gotten that clarified, we can move on!

From now on, as you embark further into your military adventure, you will remember things based on where you were at the time. Instead of saying "When I was 24 . . . " you will say, "When we were at Pope AFB . . . " I recommend looking at this as a huge advantage. Many people never leave their home state. You are now a world traveler. That is definitely sexy! Nevertheless, a move is a very stressful and emotional time for everyone. Even the most poised wife becomes a little neurotic during the big moving day. In order to minimize the hardship involved with moving, I have prepared this chapter in hopes of softening the blow. If you are already excited, you have taken the first step.

Rule Number 1

Rule number one about all moves: Your important documents are VIP members of the family. Get a briefcase or a small file holder and guard it with your life. The movers will attempt to pack them if they are left unguarded. If you are doing a DITY (Do-It-Yourself) move, you will want them organized for easy access. I cannot stress enough the importance of these things. Break this rule once and Murphy's Law will pretty much guarantee that you will never make such a disastrous rookie mistake again, ever!

I have prepared a list of important documents that are a headache to replace. Keep in mind that this is not a foolproof list. If you have a piece of paper that is not included on this list that is important and hard to replace, by all means, include it for your own safety!

Things Never to Be Forgotten

Service Records
Copy of Orders
Shot Records

Medical Records
Birth Certificates
Dental Records
Veterinary Records
Passports
Valuable Items (Needlework, jewelry or collectables that are
    irreplaceable.)
Travelers Checks
Phone numbers and Addresses
Camera and Film
Family Photos or negatives of those photos
Home Videos
Address Book
Tax and Accounting Records
List of bank account numbers and checkbooks
Power of Attorney
Marriage Certificate
Citizenship Papers
Adoption Papers
Social Security Cards for all family members
Wills
Insurance Policies
Vehicle Titles
Stock and Bond Certificates
Court Orders relating to divorce, child support, custody or alimony
Leases, deeds or mortgages
Military ID for every member of the family (over 10 years)
Resumés and letters of reference
Tax Records

* DVDs and CDs can be easily stolen during a move
* It is helpful to take a phone book from your current residence
  to avoid having to call directory assistance from your next
  town.

The Many Joys of Transportation

By now, you know that the military has an acronym for everything. The Traffic Management Office is no exception. Get used to it and learn all the ones that seem relevant. You are expected to pick this up on your own, by the way, but it is always fun to get some eye rolls and ask anyway.

TMO, Traffic Management Office. These are the movers (or office that hires your movers) that will be packing up all of your worldly possessions for each and every PCS (Permanent Change of Station), or at least the office that you need to get your funds for a DITY move.

You do have a choice about moving: not whether you move, only *how* you move. Subtle, yet crucial. One option is a DITY move, they can give you (not quite) enough money and you move your own stuff. Or, you can put your possessions in the hands of the military and pray you get it all back in one piece. But you've got a choice, as long as you are in the U.S. If you are moving overseas, they have to move you. You can't DITY to Germany. These movers are definitely one of my top ten military grievances. Movers have been known to pack (among other things) frozen meat, garbage, and suitcases with signs on them that say "Do not pack me!" I have witnessed them attempting to disassemble furniture that is not meant to be disassembled, after being told not to, no less.

Because of the movers and the unpredictability of moves, it is important to observe truth #12: *Do not acquire things that don't travel well.* This includes children and other small pets. There is nothing more annoying than spending an entire day with a car-sick child, or performing a move with him nipping at your heels. If you have a child, I recommend adoption. Really. To avoid killing him.

Also, while you are engaged in yet another cross-country road trip, the last thing you want to be concerned about is your priceless heirloom. Make no mistake, it will be broken when you get there. And while it is priceless to you, the military *will* put a price on it . . . and you won't like it.

If you think that you will not be moving too much, you are lying to yourself. Stop it. You will be moving as much as the military says. Remember his body and soul? Not his anymore.

Movers have also been known to "lose" things, mostly, the things that are irreplaceable. Even when the lost or damaged goods *are* replaceable, the military gives its members a hard time about replacing anything. Even when they do replace it, they only pay what *they* think it's worth. And obviously, they do not value it too much, as it was their people who damaged it in the first place.

Never ever allow these people to take something that you can never replace. Chances are, if you feel uneasy about letting it out of your sight, you will never see it again. Some will tell you that all you have to do to insure these belongings is be nice to the movers. This has not been my experience. Anything can happen during a move so don't take chances with things you cannot afford to gamble with.

Take these priceless things with you or leave them in storage or with a relative if you are going overseas. If you believe me and follow this advice and remain vigilant about property protection, you may be happily naïve about TMO for the rest of your life, and that's a good thing!

The "Privilege" of a DITY Move

You will make money on a DITY move! Have you heard this rumor yet? The military will pay for your movement and you will do the actual work involved with the move. This means you will move your belongings out of your house, rent a truck, put everything in it, and drive it to where you are going. This is obviously not going to happen on an overseas move, as I have said.

The only thing I find helpful about a DITY move is the fact that you will not have to be concerned with the movers breaking your possessions, which is a big plus. After that, the DITY move is highly overrated. The military will not pay you for your time, back injuries, or mental anguish. Also, you will probably make little or no profit, unless you are moving only a short distance. Even then, there are no guarantees!

A DITY move is a good idea if you are insane. Other than that, it's best to risk your precious cargo being broken to save your sanity. Either way you go, your move will be a pain in the ass. There is a trade-off for each move and it is up to you to decide what is most important to you.

Whether you choose a DITY move or a "professional" move, here are the secrets to making a move less stress oriented. If you have never moved before, copy this list and put it on your fridge. If you have moved before, this is meant to be a helpful reminder! I hope that this move will be your easiest, and that your destination is paradise. (But it's best to keep a copy of this around just in case!)

Moving Made Easier

Six Weeks Prior to move:
- Update Shot Records for you and family.
- Obtain Passports if necessary.
- Visit your Transportation Office to set up a move date and budgeting.
- Call the Chamber of Commerce and Visitors in your new town and get their new resident information packages. Learn up!
- Attempt to learn a little bit of the local language and customs if you are going overseas.
- Tentatively pack the things you may forget or that you don't want the movers to touch. Think about how to transport these items yourself.
- Set aside items that are going with you.
- Gather and update personal records file and address book. While you are doing this, you should make a list of contacts that you want to send change of address cards to once you get there.
- Remove all items from basement, storage sheds, and attics and plan a garage sale or charity donation for all items you don't want to move.
- Start using things up that you can't move, like cleaning supplies and frozen food.

- Curb your spending on frivolous items and groceries. You are only buying more things to move and give away.
- Save money for unexpected expenses that arise during a move.
- Make a list of all organizations you need to contact about your change of address.
- Complete U.S. Postal Service change of address form.
- Get copies of (or arrange for transfer at both ends of move) all school, medical, dental, veterinary, legal, military and accounting records. Reminder: It may be best to hand carry medical records.
- Contact insurance agents to transfer or cancel coverage.
- Give written notice with your realtor or the housing office.
- If you are going overseas, then things are more susceptible to break or get lost in the move. The government will pay to store items (during the tour) that you do not wish to risk moving, or think that you can live without. Antiques and crystal are good examples of things *not* to take overseas. Make arrangements for this.
- If you own a firearm, make sure the laws will allow you to take it overseas or over state lines if you plan on doing so.
- Find out if you will need to acquire an international driver's license in order to drive in your new home (overseas)

Four Weeks Prior to Move:
- Contact all current and new location utility companies (gas, water, electric, cable TV, phone & trash collection) to set connect/disconnect dates. Remember to keep current utilities hooked up until at least one day after move day. Keep the phone numbers to both utility companies handy, in case you need to contact them for changes or payment arrangements.
- Call the Housing office in your new home and inquire about the base housing list or housing assistance ("set aside" program).
- Make arrangements for relocation of pets.

- If you are packing yourself, acquire packing materials/boxes and pack items you won't need for the next month. A good place to start is the grocery store, where they will often give you boxes for free. Stockpile the good ones and pack slowly to save stress.
- If a professional mover is packing your goods, schedule packing day(s) 1 or 2 days before your actual move. You will need time to get house and affairs in order before leaving town.
- If you plan on hiring a house cleaning service, call now for an estimate and appointment. Make the appointment for a time when the house will be empty, such as the day after move day. (Cleaning services will appreciate it if the water and electricity are still on when they arrive to work. No one wants to clean in absence of the A/C.)
- Set an inspection date with your realtor or housing office. Schedule a time when you will be there to avoid being charged for nothing. In many cases, a military member must be present to set this appointment.
- Make shipping arrangements for your vehicles if you are going overseas. If you are not taking your vehicle, arrange for storage or a sale. Be sure and call your insurance company if your car will be stored; they can give you a discount on insurance.
- Have your husband make the arrangements for personal travel time during your move.
- Find out how much money you will receive (up front) for your move, especially a DITY move. They will not pay everything up front; you must make arrangements to supplement the costs.

Three Weeks Prior to Move:
- Make travel arrangements for moving trip; allow time for unexpected delays.
- Collect all important papers (listed earlier in chapter) into a small file box. It is easier to start this process early so that you will not forget something at the last minute.

- Arrange to close all local bank accounts and open new ones in new location. Make sure that your money remains accessible during the move. Acquire traveler's checks if necessary.

Two Weeks Prior to Move:
- Prepare auto(s) for trip to new home. Check your tires and have vehicles serviced. Make sure your driver's license, registration and insurance are up to date, in case you get pulled over.
- Even if your current state does not require a vehicle inspection, the next one may. Find out in advance if you will need one from your future state, you will not be allowed on base until you have one, if this is the case.
- Terminate newspaper and trash delivery services.
- Give away all plants you don't intend to move.
- Contact your TMO and confirm your arrangements.
- Return library books & rental video tapes; pick up any dry cleaning, etc.
- Make sure to settle any unpaid debts, such as traffic tickets.
- Make a Video/Photo Journal of Personal Property. Have serial numbers and owner's manuals for all big-ticket items on hand and in your personal file.
- Make sure to have Travel Request, Advance Pay, Travel Pay and DLA. These should be considered important papers and treated as such in your files.
- Confirm that your home inspection date is in place.
- Be sure to plan some fun on your trip. Maybe you can camp out while driving through the country, or visit Graceland while driving through. Make early arrangements and you can turn your move into fun.

One Week Prior to Move:
- Pack lunches or arrange for delivery on move day.
- Verify Date with movers
- Send change of address cards to family and friends, make sure that everyone knows that you are moving.

- Make plans for a baby-sitter for small children on moving day, they only get in the way.
- Make sure that everything is clean, grills, dishes, clothing, blender and microwave. You don't want to unpack dirty and messy things on the other end.
- Separate cartons and luggage items you need for personal travel and all-important items. Put them in your vehicle to keep them safest from "accidental packing" by the pros.
- Pack a box of items you will need immediately upon arrival at your new home.
- Have washer/dryer disconnected and prepared for move.
- Fill prescriptions. Have on hand 2-4 weeks' worth of medication for everyone in the family.
- Do not disconnect your telephone until the day after loading.
- Make lodging reservations.
- Have the garage sale that you planned, take excess items to the Goodwill.
- If you have not yet done so, make kennel reservations for your pets.
- Let schools know when the last day will be
- Make payment arrangements with the cleaning service.
- Overseas: You must have certificate of health from your vet in both languages, dated no less than three days prior to leaving, if you are bringing an animal.

Moving Day:

- Do not leave the movers in your home alone. Plan on supervising them all day.
- Stay with moving van driver to oversee inventory of goods.
- Make sure that nothing is disassembled that is not meant to be.
- Make sure descriptions of major items are complete on the inventory (i.e., "36-inch TV," rather than just "TV")
- Review carefully and sign inventory. Keep your copy on file until all claims have been settled.

- Keep all perishables, items not meant to be packed, food, and trash out of the movers' way. You never know what they may put in a box.
- Be sure that all cartons and loose items have a tag
- Check the inventory list from time to time to make sure all cartons are marked and clearly identified.
- Make sure boxes that contain electronics are clearly marked with a make/model and serial number
- If the inventory is inaccurate or you disagree with what the carrier has written down, tell them, and write your message on the inventory
- Do not sign anything until you have read it and agree with it.
- Do not sign for services that have not been performed.
- Make sure you get a copy of the inventory.
- Make final walk-through of your old house with the movers, including the basement, attic and closets. Make sure it's empty.
- Lock all windows and doors and drop off keys with realtor, housing office, or cleaning service.
- Make sure to pick up the kids from the sitter on the way out of town!

Overseas

So you are moving overseas! Far more of a pain in the ass than any other move . . . however, the rewards can be much greater. I envy you. Planning a move overseas requires much more preparation and hopefully, you will start a couple of months in advance. You must first read up on local culture and customs. You would not want to make a bad impression on your first day by doing something that is considered "rude." Attempt to learn the local language because you do not want to get stuck on the base in your house all the time. You should at least be able to say, "Where is the bathroom?"

Check up on the base you are going to. What is the housing situation like? What facilities will be available to you there? See if they can assign you a sponsor who has lived on the base for a while. Getting a sponsor is an opportunity to make a friend. She will also be able to help you out with preliminary concerns and may go as far as pick you up at the airport or show you around once you arrive. Keep in mind, however, that she may also forget about it and you may find that she is less than helpful or friendly.

If you are taking your vehicle, call and find out if the lien holder allows you to take it overseas with you. Many don't. If they won't, you will have to make arrangements to sell it, refinance it, or pay it off.

If possible, it's best not to take a vehicle with you at all. It might not meet the standards of the country you are entering—it was built to American standards. If you plan on shipping your vehicle, it must meet the standards by the time it gets there. Insurance is also a concern. TMO can assist you with further questions about your vehicle and shipping it. If you do ship your vehicle, make sure that there is nothing in it when you send it off. Things often disappear out of vehicles when you are shipping them. This also goes for excess equipment, such as a brush guard or chrome wheels. You may even remove the stereo, if it is worth it to you. Either way, your vehicle must be in pristine condition (a.k.a. very clean) when it arrives for shipping.

If you are planning on renting a vehicle, it might be a good idea to learn how to drive a manual transmission. Many countries drive primarily on stick shifts and it is often hard to get an automatic. You must also remember that just because you are licensed in America, it doesn't mean you will be overseas. You must find out if passing another driver's test is mandatory.

There are many challenges involved with moving overseas. Have extra money on hand in case you run into problems with the phone systems or electrical sockets. Another country is just that, and you cannot expect everything to be the same as it is here. When you get there, enjoy it. I cannot think of a single overseas location that would not have at least a few historical points of interest or fun places to shop.

Don't let the fact that you are overseas hold you back from anything. If you don't know the language, it won't kill you to try and learn it. You will find that most people are patient with you and some will speak English as well. Most of all though, treat this as an opportunity. There are so many people in this world who never travel outside their country, or spend their life savings to go to Italy. How much would they envy you?

Moving Inspections

Moving out of your current house is often the biggest pain in the ass. If you are in a military town, they will most likely keep your deposit, no matter how clean you leave your ex-house. If you are currently living on base, save yourself the pain and hire the professional cleaners to handle the inspection for you. It may be costly, but it will give you a lot less to worry about.

Learn from any mistakes you have made with this rental because you can apply that knowledge to the next. Most of all, do not kick a hole in the wall when all this frustration overcomes you.

Make sure to replace anything that you have damaged. It will be a lot cheaper for you to do it yourself than if you pay them to do it. Painting a wall does not cost $100, but they may charge you as much. Make sure that all trash is hauled away and everything is left the way you found it, including the lawn and patio.

DMV Rage

Many wonder about driver's licenses and such when moving around the country. Going to the DMV is a hassle!

You can keep your driver's license and your license plates until they expire. It is a good idea to have them match up. Your husband can renew his driver's license and registration from out of state, but you cannot. It depends on the individual state. But in either case, it is easier just to renew in the state where you are residing. In fact, it would be easier if your husband didn't bother trying to deal with an out-of-state DMV either. The DMV is hard to deal with, but they are even more so from across the country. Mail ordering a driver's license is a bigger hassle than doing so with a vehicle registration, too.

If the vehicle is in your name, you might have to deal with getting out-of-(your)state plates once yours expire. A vehicle in your husband's name can keep the out-of-state plates, but they must be kept up to date. If you want to keep your state driver's license and it is soon to expire, get it renewed while visiting your family there. Technically, you are supposed to change the states when you move anywhere for more than 6 months, but in a military town, it will go mostly unnoticed. Your insurance, however, must be changed once you get to where you are going. You must meet the state and local requirements that vary so drastically between states. This means you must prepare your budget for the financial hardship if you are moving to a high-risk city!

When your vehicle inspection sticker is expired, you may be required to get a new one. If your state does not require inspections, you may still need to get one if the state you are going to does. If your home state requires them, you may need one to renew your registration.

A state inspection is usually not a big deal and costs anywhere from $10-35. However, if your vehicle fails the inspection (because the tint is too dark, or break lights don't work, etc.), you will not be allowed to drive that vehicle on base until it can pass.

True Patriotism: You Gotta Hate the Country Sometimes

At some point during your husband's military career, you will look back on all the places that you have been. You may do this fondly, longingly, or even thankfully!

One thing I have questioned myself about over and over is: How I can love a country that is so demanding? A country that asks so much from my husband, myself, and even my children?

It's easy to love America if you're a civilian. When you are looking at that flag and know nothing about what sacrifice goes into protecting it. Sure, the flag gives you the warm feelings then! But when it comes time for you to sacrifice personally, you really have to think about it. It's hard not to be bitter at times. There are lots of warm, fuzzy sentiments about your husband protecting

America to keep it safe for your children . . . but what is that sentiment worth while he is leaving you and your children for something that seems trivial? The military always has people deployed during peace time. Is it worth the sacrifice then? What if you don't think it's important?

You may also come to ponder your husband's career as you are sitting in your worst house yet, at the worst base ever, waiting for the slowest TMO in the U.S. military to deliver your things. Hello, this is America! Ft. Hood. Look what we sacrifice to save . . . Ft. Hood. Hmm. (For those of you that have no experience with Ft. Hood, it is a desolate wasteland that might just be improved if it were bombed.) There are many military bases like this, and you will be spending your time at one (or more) of them.

You will meet the locals. Racists, ignorant, perhaps, even mean and rude people. Are these people worth your husband's life? These people who rip you off and give you military "discounts"? These ungrateful people? You will get a call from someone, the military or TRICARE saying, "That thing we said you would get? Yes, you aren't getting it now. No, we aren't sorry. Have a nice day. By the way, you owe us money and we will be taking it from your check." All these things can leave you with a sense of hopelessness that is consuming, especially when your husband is away.

You may look at the president while he is speaking on TV about how great this country is, and you may just yell at the TV, "Where? Where, Mr. President, is this great America? I would like to go there!"

Everywhere you look, there are imperfections in your country and your military life. And the president will say, "You are getting a raise." And the people will say, "No, we pay them enough." And the Congress will get a raise instead . . .

It is at this point where you need to look back on all the places you have been and think about the great things. That best friend you found in LeJeune. That great skill you learned in Carson. That great time your family had in McChord. The beautiful family you have built *in the military.* All of these are good things, and they would have been impossible without the bad.

It will strike you that you are a true American because to fully love anything, you must know and accept all of its flaws along with its weaknesses. You truly love America because you too are sacrificing for it. You accept the good along with the bad, and you (unlike others) know more about this country than anyone . . . because you have been to every godforsaken corner of it. If you haven't, just wait a while . . .

Q & A

Q. How often do duty stations change?

A. As often as the military says. You can usually expect a move every 1-3 years.

Q. What should I expect from a TMO move?

A. Nothing really, except pain, agony, and an overall loss of your will to live.

Q. What are the chances of getting to move if you put in the request?

A. Considering the fact that you *want* to move? Very small. Now, if you change your mind and you don't want to move anymore, that will increase your chances by 99 percent.

Q. I would like to just stay in one place. How long will we be in Ft. Bragg before we move, and do we have to move?

A. If you wanted to stay in one place, your husband should not have joined the military. If the military says you have to move, you *have* to move.

Q. Will my phone card work overseas?

A. Probably not; it is best to buy phone cards while you are overseas, or talk to a major phone company about a personal calling credit card.

Foreword: 10 Commandments of the Base

1. Thou shall flash your military ID at the gate. You will only need your military ID at the front gate if it is inaccessible to you. If it is in your hand, you will be waved right through.
2. Thou shalt never park at the front of the lot. There are no handicapped spaces; the handicapped spaces are replaced with high-ranking officer spaces. You'll notice that they are always empty because if you are an officer of this status, you can basically park right in front of the store where it says No Parking. And anyway, these high-ranking men send their aides to shop.
3. Thou shall sweat in July and freeze in December without complaint. The military feels that air-conditioning in military facilities is not required, especially in the middle of summer.
4. Thou shall tip all baggers whom the gov underpays. Remember that the people at the commissary bag your groceries for "free." They will expect you to tip them. If you don't tip them, you will be chastised and made to feel "cheap." You are expected to learn this by example, or through your own mistakes.
5. Honor thy ID Card. You will need your military ID on base for everything.
6. Honor thy military rent-a-cops. People drive like maniacs. But if you do this, you will be ticketed. A base ticket is a pain in the ass. Just be slow, but not too slow, you wouldn't want to get a ticket for that. Always remember that the military police are very bored! Like all men, they want any excuse to play with their lights.
7. Thou shall not go to base on payday. Paydays are the worst for crowds.
8. Thou shall not taunt the guards. No, they do not find it amusing if you say you might have some "contraband" as they are searching your vehicle. Don't piss them off. They have M16s, you know.
9. Thou shall not drive up the down aisle in the commissary

with the cart. You will get in trouble.

10. Thou shall not show affection to thy husband on base. There is nothing more obnoxious than standing in line behind the girl who is clinging to her husband like a scared puppy. If your husband is in uniform, this is unacceptable. If he is in civilian attire, it's still not attractive. You are an independent woman, act like it!

CHAPTER 8

Welcome to Your New Base

Find Your New House

You have arrived! Welcome to your new home for a while. Note your first impression of your new place immediately. Murphy's Law will always prevail when predicting your next move. If you hate this place and you want to move, odds are that you will be stuck there for years on end. On the other hand, if you love your new station and wish to stay there forever, expect to move soon. The military will not tolerate your happiness.

Your first order of business (after finding a place to stay temporarily) is to find more permanent living arrangements. The cost of living varies greatly from one base to another, so you will be assured that the housing prices will be a shock to you. The BAH (Basic Allowance for Housing) also varies from base to base, but it will not always cover your living costs.

Contact the housing office if you have not already. If you are looking to rent a house or apartment, they can help you immensely. They are, after all, the authorities, and they know what's out there. As you know, everyone is eager to do business with the military.

Once you find a home that is acceptable, the housing office can help you set up an allotment. The rent will automatically be deducted from your check, one-half on the first of the month and the other on the fifteenth. They will also waive or lower the deposit. This comes in very handy when you are on a budget (and aren't we all!).

I cannot stress enough how helpful this housing service is. Even if you are planning to live in base housing, they can help you find alternative housing until your name reaches the top of the list. Always contact the housing office first!

Nasty House

All bases differ. But the needs of people at the base generally don't. Once you arrive at your first base, you will want to acquire housing almost immediately. Most people don't have the time and money to secure a house beforehand. If you choose military housing, you are basically gambling. Most people can't get on the housing list until they have orders in hand. This means that you will be dealing with whatever is first available. The wait for housing can last anywhere from five minutes to a year or two.

Even if base housing is full, the housing office can still offer you assistance in finding housing in town, as mentioned before. With these, you might really be gambling. No matter what the case may be, sometimes, you will get a palace and sometimes you will get a dump. Most often though, you will get a dump.

Truth #8 *You are moving to the ghetto.* I cannot explain to anyone the shock value of walking into your brand-new house and realizing that it is a dump. The industrial tile (in base homes) does much justice to the "ghetto look." If living in a house that always looks and feels dirty is going to bother you, you may want to consider a divorce now.

It is virtually impossible to live on the housing allotment without supplementing it with your own pay. Since you live in a military town, it will be more expensive to rent a house that is typical for the area. Even then, the rental properties usually aren't much better than base housing. It is advisable for the lower ranks to live with the tile on base.

Everyone I know who has gotten out of the military has acquired more surface area rugs than they can ever possibly utilize. This is because of the aforementioned tiles in base homes. Even rental houses need to be personalized and area rugs are an easy way to accomplish this.

Don't fret. Even the nastiest houses can be made into a home.

Any house feels more home-like once you are comfortable. Comfort is the first order of business after getting the electricity and water turned on. Your house will feel much less like a home if you have unpacked boxes lying around for months. Get unpacked as quickly as possible, and deal with decorating last.

I have found that it is not the house that makes the home, it's the people and things inside it. No matter how unfamiliar you are with your surroundings, it will be your home as long as your family remains there. This is your sanctuary from the outside world, no matter how leaky the roof may be. Keep calling those maintenance guys; they'll get around to you. Remember, "Home is where the military sends you."

Pros and Cons of Base Housing

You may be confused (as many are) about how base housing "works." So I will use this opportunity to explain it in the best way I can. My number one thought—if you want to live on base, put your name on the list *now*. Housing lists are the main reason people generally live in civilian quarters.

Keep in mind that a base house contains only the basics. Different bases have different qualities in housing and you can easily find out about yours by asking around or visiting the base's website. The higher the rank, the higher the quality of quarters (supposedly). The best qualities about an officer's house as opposed to an enlisted house is a screened patio, maybe a car port and perhaps, if you're lucky, a dishwasher. All in all, "free" is not a bad price for these homes. You must weigh the cost of living in the area when making the choice between base housing and civilian housing. In some places, like Hawaii, for example, the cost of living may greatly exceed your BAH. This is when it is advisable to live on the base.

Your BAH or housing allowance is included in your husband's paycheck to cover the cost of rent, electricity, and water in your home. Living on base, you will not receive this money because all of these things will be provided to you. Sometimes, you make money and sometimes, you lose money by living on (or off) base. The best way to find out is to talk to someone in the area about it.

If you opt for base, remember that you may have to live in town for a while before a base house is made available to you, anyway. Also, many leases will not release you from your responsibility just because your name reached the top of the base housing list.

You can set a "target" date for when you would like your housing made available, but there are never any guarantees. You can also ensure yourself a place on the list (without being called) by going on "inactive" status. This will hold your place in line without committing you to take the house when your name reaches the top. You can call and put yourself on "active" status at any time. When your name reaches the top, they will call you. You may or may not get to look at different houses and choose. It differs between commands, although you are supposed to be able to choose. Either way, most of the base housing looks the same, with only a couple different floor plans anyway. If you get a newly remodeled home, you have won the lottery! (You also won't learn much about the military's attitude until you have lived in one of the more ghetto-ish homes.)

The number of bedrooms in your home will be determined by the military. They will evaluate your husband's number of dependents and decide if your two young sons can share a room or not. This is a long drawn out process and it is just as ridiculous as any other military decision. There is no use in arguing with them unless their ruling is certifiably insane. Then you might have a 2 percent chance of getting what you want. Usually, beggars can't be choosers.

Keep in mind that, while living on base, there are responsibilities that you agree to. One, for instance, is mowing the lawn frequently. They can also restrict the number of pets you keep. You will be under the jurisdiction of the MPs (Military Police) rather than local or state police. And it is sometimes difficult to get guests on the base when they are visiting your home, especially if they don't have an ID card.

The military is allowed to inspect your home at any time.

This seems to make people nervous and uncomfortable. In reality, *any* landlord can inspect his property at his leisure. Odds are, if you leave the military alone, they will leave you alone. Keep your yard tidy and trash free and you will probably be safe from these horrible violations of privacy. Your neighbors will all be in a similar situation as you, so it may be easier to make friends. However, it might also be easy to get involved with the base gossip mill or to be ridiculed by it.

The biggest complaint of these women seems to be other wives who mow their lawn in skimpy clothes while their husbands are deployed. They hate these women because they have a good body and are showing it off, "forcing" other women's husbands to look. This is the biggest complaint I have ever heard. Really!

All in all, living on base can be a pain. I do recommend that everyone do it at least once, just to get a good feel for military life. If you really want to experience hardcore military, this is the place for you.

For those Choosing Base

Truth # 14: *Uniformity is Crucial.* In the military, perfection is the key. This applies to everything, not only uniforms. While your husband is at work being inspected, you will be slaving away, preparing your yard for inspection by the base Yard Nazis.

If you think that mowing is your only requirement, you are sadly mistaken. Your grass must be kept at a quarter-inch length. Depending on where you live, this could require 2-3 mows a week!

As for your hedges, trim them often and use a ruler if possible! Do you think it would be okay to keep a chair on your porch? Guess again! Never, and I repeat, *never* use new wood bark that does not match the old dirty wood bark already in place in your yard! And please let me know if you find any of the dirty kind for sale.

If it rains one day and you are unable to perform your yardly duties, it's okay. But, the communists will be at your door the following day, wondering why you didn't have the foresight to tend the yard the day before it rained. Hint: They watch the news and they always know if rain is predicted. They expect that you also have nothing better to do than watch the news.

Keeping the base homes all looking alike is a big job. You *will* be harassed for not doing your part! I suggest considering therapy if you decide to move on base. The Prozac will save you a lot of frustration!

Buying a Pain in the Ass

When a young couple gets married, one of their first big purchases is usually a house. Unfortunately, this is, for the most part, a long-term goal for a military couple. Most military families live in a constant state of instability due to deployments, finances and moves. Although some choose to purchase a house at their first duty station, it's just not a good idea.

There are some inherent problems with purchasing a house that some do not think about when they make this choice. It is true that you can sometimes find nicer living accommodations through ownership than through renting. But most rental homes are perfectly acceptable for living in, as well as being more economical. Some feel that they are "wasting" their money when renting and prefer to put their money towards something that will build equity.

While there is nothing wrong with wanting to buy a home, equity is something that probably will not happen if the military moves you in a year or two, and this is a definite possibility. No matter how stable you may think your orders are, there will always be the chance of a military wild card. You can never be too sure about anything in the military. Buying a home is a permanent solution to a very short-term problem.

There is also the possibility of a long deployment or unaccompanied tour. If your husband is deployed for 6 months or a year, will you want to remain living in your new home, far from your family? Chances are, you won't.

Many wives instead choose to go home and be close to family during such a difficult separation. If this happens, do you want to attempt paying rent in your hometown, as well as a mortgage?

Usually, the military does not provide enough (financially) to make such a feat possible. So you will be stuck either living there or attempting to sell your home while there is little equity in it, and probably losing money.

Of course, there is also the chance that your husband will be "permanently changing stations." If this happens, you will be forced to rid yourself of your new home—again, while there is little equity in it. Until it sells, there will be no extra money in your budget for anything. Also, it is usually quite difficult to sell even the greatest house in a military town because most military families make the wise choice to rent.

So, you may decide to rent your home out. This means that you will be leaving a property manager in charge of making sure that the new tenants treat your home as well as you did. Any damage that occurs in the home will be your responsibility. Also, tenants have been known to tear down wallpaper and paint walls funky colors, not to mention the fact that pet damage alone can exceed any deposit you may ask for.

Adding to the constant worry is the fact that you will be helpless to check up on your home, unless you want to pay an ungodly price to fly over just to "drop by," which will not be appreciated. Also, if no one wants to rent because the house is not marketable or is too expensive, you will be left with the financial burden that is your dream home. When all is said and done, it pays to rent. It will save you a lot of frustration when conducting your next move, which is already going to be stressful. Surely, if the military wanted you to buy a home, they would issue you one.

Although many argue that renting is "paying someone else's mortgage," you are paying for the added convenience of being able to leave at a moment's notice and have no chains holding you to a base that you probably don't care much for, anyway. Financially and mentally, renting is just the best option, as long as your husband remains in service.

When You Arrive

- Check in with TMO as soon as you get to your new duty station and give them a contact phone number; this way, you can receive your belongings as soon as they arrive. If they catch you at home when your things come into town, they can deliver immediately, meaning you will not have to wait an extra two weeks (or more) for them to deliver.
- Take photos of damages in your new home as well as inventorying it. Give copies to the landlord. This will make the move-out inspection much easier someday.
- Know which rooms you are going to want your large items placed in and let the movers know ahead of time.
- Carefully check each item off the inventory list after it is removed from the truck; make sure everything is there.
- Check all items for damage. This is very important; they must be noted by the movers in order for you to place a claim.
- List any damaged or missing items on the inventory sheet *before* you sign it and allow them to leave.
- Do not sign for anything that you don't understand or did not happen.
- The movers must put together and unpack anything you ask, or everything. They will not do this if you don't know they are required to. If there is anything that you want them to assemble or unpack, let them know and see that it is done.

Once you have discovered what is to be your new home, you now have to do . . . everything else! While waiting for TMO to deliver your goods or while you are in the process of moving in your own goods, you must hook up all of the utilities. This is where the extra money for deposits and such comes in very handy.

If you find yourself short, check with your bank and find out if they will give you a waiver in order to save you the deposit. (They will only do this if they like your credit and the company will accept it.) If you find yourself lacking and your bank will not help, check with the finance office to see if they will grant you an advance in your husband's pay. If none of these things are working for you, check with one of the military relief societies for an interest-free loan. If you are again refused, you must go to a local check cashing or military loan institution. Be sure to bring an LES and only borrow what is needed, the interest rates are very high.

If you have yet to make a banking choice or are confused about banking, check out on-line banks like USAA (www.usaa.com). USAA will cater to your needs as a military family. Whatever you decide, the worst thing you can do is use a local armed services bank, such as Marine Federal or Army Federal Credit Union. These banks are in business to rip off the military, and they do not have worldwide ATM locations.

If you have overlooked things during your move, you can go to the local relocation assistance office to borrow household goods until yours arrive, or until you can buy some. You can also get information about your new place and find people to answer your questions. This is essentially the "welcome wagon."

Once you have taken care of finances, you may be concerned about other things while getting settled. Start by familiarizing yourself with the facilities and programs offered on the base. If you have not yet enrolled in DEERS at the TRICARE office, it will be good to take care of that immediately. The paperwork will take a couple of months and you never know when you will need treatment.

If you are interested in being employed, you can utilize the Family Member Employment Assistance Program. Contact Career Resources for more information. They may be able to assist you in finding a job on the base, as well as in the economy. Until you are employed, you may want to spend some time at the Volunteer Center. Volunteering looks good on a resumé, and it kills time.

If schooling is more to your tastes, you can make use of the Life-Long Learning Program. They can assist you with college applications and tell you about any grants or scholarships that you may qualify for. They can also assist you in setting up a SAT or ACT test, along with a multitude of other services. If you are college bound, it is definitely worth checking out.

Base Finance

They say that military benefits make up for lack of pay. Maybe, this is true in theory, but I have found that the benefits don't help you out much when the water bill arrives. This being said, I believe that the only thing that can make up for lack of pay is budget planning (or more money). If you are young, you may believe that you can handle it all. I sure did. Different places have drastically varying prices on things. I have paid anywhere from $20-200 per month in different areas just for electricity. Prices are highly inflated in military towns, not just on electricity, but on everything. Many fail to recognize this. And if you are currently stationed somewhere where the prices aren't so bad, don't get too comfortable. Reminder: When you fail to plan for something like a PCS, it will hit you at the worst possible time.

Before acquiring any new debt, go to the local base finance office and have them create a budget for you. Read finance books and do whatever you need to do to keep your head above water. Some people live happily in the military with great financial freedom, while others struggle immensely. Either way, those great benefits won't bail you out when you get into trouble.

Don't Knock My Home

Upon arrival at your new home, you will most likely form your own opinions about the place. You may love it or hate it, or even be indifferent to it. If your opinion is negative, it will probably offend the locals. Try not to share it with them. People get highly sensitive over places, as ridiculous as that seems.

I once found myself in an e-mail conversation with an Air Force wife stationed in California. I felt that she was so fortunate to have such a great duty station. I have high regards for the West

Coast and desperately wanted to return there while stationed in North Carolina. I mentioned my current state to her and told her my opinions on the area. In my opinion, the entire southeast seems to hold themselves on some sort of religious pedestal, not allowing the sale of liquor on Sunday and so forth—trying to legislate morality. The state of North Carolina does not allow gambling, but they do allow in the law for cousins to marry. What is that about?

The school system is sorely lacking in good teachers and computers, as well as textbooks and other such things. I mentioned to her that if they allowed gambling in the state, maybe they could get a better budget for education.

Her response was very snooty and the bottom line was that she was from North Carolina and she did not appreciate me "knocking her home." Leave it to the spoiled Air Force to get upset so easily over something so petty.

She seemed to have no problems knocking the West Coast at all, since they (on the West Coast) are "completely devoid of morals at all." Thank God! I have heard many people make comments about my home in Washington state, or the West Coast in general. I cannot argue that it does not rain a lot or that the drivers aren't on the brink of insanity. In fact, my sister-in-law drives rather madly. I usually laugh off criticism of my home.

I have never gotten upset over people knocking any of the places they have lived (including the places that I consider home.). If they are living there, they have the right to an opinion about the place as much as anyone else. Living somewhere that you were not raised clears your vision about that place somewhat.

Often, the military folks have more accurate opinions about the places they have lived simply because they are not blinded by sentiment. This girl was obviously missing North Carolina so badly that she could not focus enough on the fact that all I was saying was that I didn't care for North Carolina. Maybe, those school systems really do need a larger budget if they pumped this girl out.

Since nothing can ever compare to your home, this truth applies. Truth #15: *There is no such thing as a good duty station or post.* Everyone hates their duty stations because no one is at home there. Usually, even if the station does qualify as home, it is disliked. Nothing compares to home, and that is the truth. Getting used to living in shithole towns in the middle of nowhere is a part of getting used to the military. The military chooses these places totally at random, but only when the land is cheap. I am often impressed by the military's ability to find the worst places on earth to position a base.

They buy this land because it is cheap. They will have men build their offices and public buildings using only the best supplies. Then, they will contract civilians to build your base housing at a low cost.

Getting Ripped Off

No discussion about a military base is complete without mentioning this topic. You almost certainly *have* to get ripped off at least once in life. I make it a practice to avoid this when possible. I never speak to telemarketers or door-to-door salespeople, or became interested in "free gift" gimmicks. I also never shop at the local car dealerships because of their inflated prices; I look for deals in the commissary and shop primarily at Wal-Mart.

Yep, I was pretty smart. I never saw it coming. At last, I decided to get professional photos taken of my family. Not at Sears, but by a *real* photographer. He came to our house and unloaded thousands of dollars worth of equipment. He had previously been in the Navy, he was friendly, and he seemed trustworthy. He took beautiful photographs. When we perused the proofs, we became overly excited by the quality of work.

We chose our shots and paid him almost $300 up-front, not to mention the sitting fee. He smiled and promised us our photos as soon as possible and walked out our front door. We never saw him again.

The check had cleared before I started becoming suspicious. Phone call after phone call, I became more and more frustrated and frantic. I got his home number and tried harassing him, until my attempts became so futile that I was torturing myself more than I was him. Sure enough, he already had a record with the Better Business Bureau.

I could have taken him to court were it not that we were in the process of moving. I'd like to blame it on the military, but the base just attracts these vultures. Young servicemen seem to put dollar signs in the eyes of civilians, although I don't know why they think these men have any money.

Before employing any services, acquire a list of reputable and irreputable businesses in the area from the military Consumer Affairs office. These businesses will have a record if they have been doing bad business with military folks. Often, this is your only recourse; no business wants to be blacklisted by the military.

I tried the Better Business Bureau, the Photographers of America and even the phone book in an attempt to get him unlisted for his crime. I feel horrible that he is out there, ripping off other young servicemen who could be worse off than my family. The moral of the story is to always keep a watchful eye (especially in military towns), and never pay for anything in advance.

Your Safety

Many wives have an unreasonable illusion about safety while living on base. Even when living off-base, wives are plagued by an unusual attitude about the safety of a base. I cannot stress enough how dangerous this mindset is.

When you enter a base, you must have proper authorization, or you must fill out a piece of paper. As it is, this is a pain. However, it does not stop unauthorized persons from gaining access to your base. The military conducts car searches and ID checks. Usually, the only thing they find is illegal drugs on their servicemen. The idea that a civilian cannot come on base is absurd. Many civilians work on the base. Although a civilian usually has no reason or interest to enter the base, it is possible.

As simple as this may seem to you, I find that many "crusty old wives" have unreasonable expectations that the base is (and *should* be) entirely secure. Neither is true. How much freedom are you willing to give up for the illusion of safety? The truth is, although the base provides some protection, base security is a joke.

If a terrorist wants to blow you up, they will, regardless of what precautions you are taking. September 11 and the attack on Pearl Harbor are prime examples of backdoor attacks. The fact is, neither would have been prevented by increased security on military bases.

A simpler example is the ADT alarm system I have in my home. I do use it. I set it even when I am in the house. It makes me feel good and fuzzy inside. It gives me an illusion of safety. However, if someone wants to get me, they will wait until I am taking out the trash or walking to the mailbox. If not, they could easily use a ladder to reach a second-story window that the alarm does not cover. I know this and I am aware of it.

The point? If someone wants to get you, they will, base security be damned, ADT be damned. The reason you should not believe that you are safe is because it causes you to let your guard down. Your safety is *your* responsibility. The military doesn't care about your safety, they are protecting their interests, not yours. So maybe, the bombs on your base are secure. You are not.

If you remember that safety is your responsibility, you will be safer because you will practice safe habits. Never leave it up to some MP at the front gate. That takes away your control and you are giving up accountability for your personal well-being.

Do you need to be paranoid? No. You need to be aware.

CHAPTER 9

Day-to-Day Life in the Mafia

Military Enigma

Most people don't care to know about military life. The family alone knows the sacrifice the military requires. You may find that even your own parents are insensitive or do not understand your new life.

Growing up in a military home was hard. The military was a faceless institution that controlled everything in our lives. Big Brother didn't *have* to watch us . . . Big Brother *controlled* us. The only aspect of our lives that they did not control was our humor, and that's why it thrived.

You may find it hard to accept the fact that someone else is controlling your life. This is completely normal. The military is something families grow to loathe . . . or love. The thing that is so difficult about this loathing is that it is hard to loathe anything in particular, other than the abstract word "military."

After giving this much thought, I have come to compare the military to the Mafia. Like the Mafia, the military works on a rank system. The military has a godfather (the president) who makes all the rules and gives all of the commands. After the godfather gives these orders, his right-hand men relay the message through the chain of command. Shit rolls downhill and always has—in the military, the shit jobs go to the lowest-ranking man. Don't be surprised when your husband has been out of boot camp for exactly ten minutes when he is doing someone else's shitwork. This will continue until he is out of the military, or he works his way to the rank of "president."

The Mafia's lowest-ranking men are always the ones who do the shitwork. They perform the most menial and dangerous tasks and they reap the fewest benefits and rewards. When the police come to scoop someone up, they get this guy. Coincidentally, this is also the guy who has the least knowledge about what is actually going on. Often, the godfather knows nothing about what has happened to this poor man who is just doing his job. There is seldom any recognition. Such is the military and (usually) life.

Also, the Mafia holds itself responsible for running things. If anything goes wrong, someone must be "extinguished." If you think this is not the case in the military, just wait a while. Although they do not technically "off" anyone, they have managed to inflict punishments that are almost as bad. I encourage you in the future to think about how "Mafia-like" the military really can be. I think that with every military encounter, you will come to believe this more and more. No one wants to believe that their loved one is an indentured servant, but that is all your husband is to them, just like if he had joined the Mafia. And one day, they will ask him to do them a favor . . .

Uniform Code of Military Justice (UCMJ)

You may not ever hear much about the good old UCMJ. The UCMJ is a special list of rules that applies only to the military. These are the laws that govern military life. No discussion about the military is complete without this being included.

These are important rules, like not being disrespectful to an officer (removing his freedom of speech), absence without leave (removing his right to the reasonable pursuit of happiness) and so on. I highly recommend that you read the UCMJ, it is quite amusing. It says things like "You are not allowed to rape any female who is not your wife."

The part of the UCMJ that is important to everyone is Article 125: Sodomy. This is important because while in boot camp, they very clearly explain this article to you. The military defines sodomy as any "unnatural carnal copulation." They go on to explain that any sexual position other than missionary is against the rules. Of course, my favorite: Absolutely no oral sex of any kind. Despite Bill Clinton's blatant example to the contrary, BJs *do* count. Well, they do in the military . . . as long as you are not the president. So, until your husband is elected, beware.

After they finished explaining this to me (in boot camp), the room was dead silent. We were all dumbfounded. The same question ran through all of our heads. "Are they really going to check?" The instructor piped up at this point and gave us an answer.

"What you do in your bedroom is your business. Keep it private."

I guess its another one of the military's "don't ask, don't tell" policies. You can do anything as long as you are not caught. You should probably refrain from doing "it" anywhere you could be caught with your pants down, so to speak. I can think of no more embarrassing charge for your husband to deal with than "sodomy" on his permanent record. Well, maybe he won't be embarrassed, but you sure will! Yes, the record does follow him *everywhere*, by the way!

I know your mind is still running. Let me say that it is impossible for the military to monitor everyone's sex life. They just aren't going to do it. So unless you are caught having sex on the third deck in the hallway of the barracks (and get caught by the guard), you are pretty much okay.

Do I do these things? Of course not! But you aren't supposed to ask . . .

SIQ

Out with the old and in with the new! Say goodbye to the days of calling in sick! In the military, you have to drag yourself to work unless you are dead . . . and even then, you better have a pretty good excuse for dying without permission! It is true what I say: "If the military wanted you to have sick days, they would have issued them to you!"

Back to your husband dragging himself into work, he will have to go to sick call and wait for a while, probably for a long while. Then, a doctor or medic will see him for five minutes and the decision will be made. Hopefully a good one. With any luck, your husband will be home by late morning to rest up for his SIQ (Sick in Quarters) time.

Believe it or not, I have found that this flawless system doesn't work half as well as it should. Leave it up to the government to make a decision and you can pretty much guarantee they will make it wrong. This leads directly to men puking while running PT. Hopefully, right on the shoes of the medic who pronounced him healthy. There is nothing more entertaining than when people get what they deserve. Too bad this happens so infrequently.

The Pork Chop Platoon

Your husband will be required to perform in the Physical Fitness (PT or PFT) test and pass it. The standards change over the years based on his age, meaning it will get "easier" when he's an old fogie. He will also have to maintain his weight according to the military height and weight chart (which is based on his sex, age and height). While the PT test is not hard for most, it is often difficult for some to meet the standards.

Wives often complain when their husbands are unable to perform during the PT. She will get mad at the military and then claim that the standards are unfair. Her husband will be put onto the military's diet and exercise program in order to lose weight, or until he can meet the fitness standards. My husband lovingly refers to this program as the "Pork Chop Platoon."

The government may not be sympathetic about the challenges involved with weight loss, but by God, they do have a program for it! If your husband is physically unfit or too fat, he may end up in the so-called Pork Chop Platoon. It doesn't matter if he is unfit because he has been on a ship for 6 months. It is his job to be fit, and by the way, they do have a gym on most naval ships.

Try not to complain too much. If he does not do well in the PCP, the military might just kick him out of the service all together. An unfit soldier is just as useless to them as, say . . . a complaining wife! Now is the time to encourage your slightly obese husband. Why not offer to get up and run with him instead of complaining about how unfair everything is? Always remember that it could be worse; he could be in the Marine Corps. The Marines, by far, have the most challenging requirements during PT.

Nevertheless, every service member is important. Every member of the service must be fit and competent to be sent to war. The Navy does not just ride in ships and the Air Force does other things besides just fly in planes (I think). Physical fitness is important not only so that they can do their jobs, but also to stay healthy. You do not want an enemy sniper picking him out of the crowd because he is the largest target.

Promotion Board

After your husband has been in and settled for a while, he will suddenly discover that he has been put up on a "board." This is the promotion board (although it is not always for a promotion) and it is another big, fat, painfully involved military ceremony. However, this is an obstacle that must be dealt with positively, if you ever want him to make more money. He may come home with his little booklet of questions. He will prepare his uniforms. He will attach and re-attach the collar pins (and other junk) between six and twenty times to get them perfect. He will use a ruler for the other stuff. He will iron everything and make sure nothing is stained. (Too bad he did not even go through this much trouble for the wedding!)

During this time, you will be quizzing him on the firing time of a specific weapon or asking what general was in charge during the battle of this and such. After he has completed his uniform, he will practice the "drill." Military bearing, standing up straight, "Lcpl. Gettinger reporting to . . . blah blah blah."

What he is learning is not important, except to the military (who cares about them?). What *you* are learning is important. This is the true military. This is what they do. It is probably the only time you will get a glimpse of his work life while he is at home. It is also one of the few opportunities that you will get to actually help him with something, so take advantage of it. Which bring us to Truth # 16: *Ceremony is more important than life itself.* Much like the military follows moronic policies for no good reason, they also have some stupid ceremony for everything. Colonel is retiring? Let's have a retirement ceremony! Sailor broke his leg? Let's have a ceremony for that too. What the heck?

First, they gather all the important guys and put them on a podium. Then, they get all the insignificant guys (like your husband) to waste their time marching in circles. Keep in mind that these actions would never be performed during an actual war . . . I hope.

Really, it is about the male ego and stroking it. That is about it.

If your husband would like for you to be a spectator at one of these events, be grateful. If you have not seen it a gigajillion times before, it may actually be interesting to you this once. But take it from me, if you have seen one, you have seen them all . . . but don't tell my husband I said that! Every woman in those bleachers will feel the same way that you do. I mean, they can't tell which one their husband is either, for God's sakes! And no one really cares. They probably all want to go home. I recommend tying a colored ribbon on your husband so you can tell him apart from the others (in secret, and somewhere he can't see!) The same as you do on your luggage to tell it apart from the other black suitcases.

Useless ceremonies, but those men will still practice for them! During one of these "board drills" in my home, I had a neighbor come over to ask me what the hell was going on in our house. She complained of what she thought was constant yelling and was concerned that we were fighting. Alas, I told her that we were not fighting. The yelling she heard was coming from my husband while practicing his cadence and drill. "Left . . . FACE! forward . . . MARCH!" Your husband might be fortunate enough to get promoted during a board. However, when he does, he will be put on a list. Based on his performance, he gets a number on the list. Whenever a billet for that rank opens up, the person at the top of the list will pin on and start getting paid. For this reason, the process can take months. Like everything else in the military, you need to wait for the new money.

Med Board

I have tried to explain it over and over, yet I still cannot make it clear enough. The military doesn't care about anyone. They care about their objectives, whatever those may be. I suspect that the objective is advancing their own careers. For this reason, they aren't family friendly. They need your husband to do a job, and if he is unable to perform, he will be of no use. If he is of no use, he will be promptly discarded like an old pair of shoes.

If they discover a problem with your husband, they will put him on a medical board. Like a promotion board *ceremony*, he will be up for scrutiny in front of the bigwigs. They will decide his fate based on the color of his tail feathers.

I met a woman with a husband who did desk work in the Air Force. She was mighty concerned because he had suddenly developed diabetes. She wondered if he was to be kicked out. She liked having him in the Air Force, and they had planned on him going career. Unfortunately, they only take healthy people for a reason. I hardly think that it would be rational to send a man with diabetes to war. If he fell into a diabetic coma, odds are he would die. That would cost the military money, and that would be bad for them. What were the chances of her husband going to war? Slim to none, if you ask her. He could still perform his desk work and function normally in day-to-day military life. For this, she reasoned, he should stay in. But it doesn't matter what she reasoned, the military made their own decision. No one ever really cares for the military's decisions. Every service member is expected to be able to perform in the field without being hindered by physical conditions. For this reason, there is no room for the weak. It's not nice and it's not fair. But they usually shoot the weak sheep. Survival of the fittest has never been pretty. However, a medical board, like a promotion board, can take months. If this happens to you, start making arrangements and saving money just in case your husband is booted.

Duty

Duty, ah yes, its an American tradition. No, not that dream about soiling your pants in public . . . that would be *doodie*! I'm talking about staying up all night, living it up and . . . watching the head! While the base is peacefully sleeping, someone must remain awake to guard the fort, so to speak. This never happens at home, only at the base. My husband comes home and passes out. We may have some attacking cockroaches, but other than that . . . we are relatively unguarded. Those noises that go "bump in the night" usually go unnoticed by my husband, as well as the cockroaches, which is a perfect illustration for why someone needs to guard these sleeping soldiers, airmen, Marines and seamen. Okay, and answer the phone too. Yes, your husband will be away for the night. Depending on his rank, he may never face duty. If you are not so lucky, he will get it anywhere from once a month to once a week (and even as much as three times a week), depending on how many people they have to choose from. It is also used as punishment.

It will be assigned at "random" on a volunteer basis, and he usually will have no choice with the voluntary part. Not surprisingly, duties usually fall on the most inconvenient nights possible, like during his leave. He can be put on the duty roster smack dab in the middle of that Hawaii vacation!

If he is unable to make it, he can pay someone to cover for him, or call in a favor if he knows anyone willing to suffer. But if no one shows, he is ultimately responsible. Duties are long and lonesome and usually consist of staying up all night and walking the quiet corridors, parking lots or even bathrooms . . . OKAY! And answering the phone!

Don't fret, visitors are allowed! Many a wife has frequented the duty shack in the wee hours of the night to make a conjugal visit to her husband . . . and bring him dinner. For some, this is fun and exciting . . . the dinner too. Technically, females are not allowed in the barracks after a certain time, but the only people guarding the barracks from these evil females are, well . . . your husband and his buddies. I'm sure they won't care, though.

If your husband is in the Navy, you might have a little trouble getting on the ship, I suppose. But think of how much fun you could have shouting at him from the pier. You would definitely have a quick audience, and that is for sure. Or you could just call him, whatever. If you are a stickler for rules and don't like getting caught with your pants down (no pun intended), there are other methods. Going to the base at dinnertime is perfectly acceptable and bringing an innocent meal is always appreciated—as long as you are out by curfew. In any case, duty is just another part of military life that will be dealt with. While it is hard on your husband, hey, you get a night off! Congratulations, and here's to you looking forward to all the nights off you will have to come!

Emergency Leave

My husband's mother had passed away. Despite his grief, he took care of things in a timely manner. The plane trip from North Carolina to Washington state was an especially difficult financial strain for us. But he had to go. A day later, everything was set. His emergency leave had been granted and the ticket had been purchased.

Murphy's Law never fails to kick in at times like this. The first snowstorm we had ever seen during our entire three years in North Carolina occurred that very day. I'm sure I'll never see anything like that again (until there is another family emergency).

We got in a car accident due to the black ice on the way to the airport. And inevitably, the flight had been cancelled. When he finally did board the plane, it sat on the ground for hours before taking off, only to leave him stranded in St. Louis for two days due to a cancelled connection. At last, he arrived in Washington, rather rumpled, I'm certain. One day after his arrival and before the funeral, he was called back and his leave was revoked.

"Report back immediately, you're going to Cuba." He was

told by his MSgt. He did as he was told, rushing back in the wake of the storm and missing his mother's funeral. The deployment left for Cuba an hour before his plane landed.

Nothing is certain, not even emergency leave or deployments. Service members are in the military 24/7. They can be called at any time and they are at the mercy of our government and the people who run it. Much like God, the military giveth and the military taketh away.

The E-5 Ulcer

I always thought that when my husband moved up in rank, things would get easier. And they did . . . financially. Around the time he hit E-5, he began having constant stomach and back pains. He stopped getting home at 4:30 P.M. and started coming home later and later. I guess I never thought that with increased pay, there would be increased responsibility to match. Many men have trouble adapting during the transition, from following orders to belting them out.

My husband rapidly developed an ulcer. The more miserable he got, the more responsibilities they piled on him, the more late-night phone calls came in, and the more sleep he needed.

In turn, I too, developed stress pains. "What time should I put dinner on?" "Will he be here to tuck the baby in?" "Where the fuck is my husband?"

A great (and essential) lesson in military life: "Don't sweat the small stuff." Nothing is so important as to damage your health.

In time, we adapted. I waited until he got home to put dinner on and he stopped answering the phone. Things got easier. But it is a good reminder to always empathize with our leaders. I would never want to be in the shoes of our president, disagreeing with him as I may. I would like to be a presidential advisor, however. Being a leader is a far harder job than being a follower. We forget that when leaders seem to be unfair or cranky. My husband finally realized that his leaders are people, too.

But as my husband's stress rolled down to me, I'm sure it did on the men in his charge also. Shit rolls downhill in the military, and it ends up on the wives.

The Bad Word: "Re-enlistment"

There will come a time in every military career where the question will be posed. It has become a question that sits on all of our minds, like some sort of demon waiting to attack us if we answer incorrectly. The question is: to re-enlist or not? Frequently answered with a bunch of "What ifs?"

There are many pros and cons on both sides of this argument. Overall, it is something that your family will have to decide together based on your personal circumstances. All the new military wives say "We will never re-enlist and we would get out now if we could." This answer oftentimes changes over the years. In fact, I find that the women who jump to this conclusion are the ones who do end up as veteran wives (crusty or otherwise).

If you do decide to re-enlist, you can get a way better deal. Make sure that you and your husband make a list of things that are important to you—and make sure you have a contract that says the military will give you those things in exchange for another 4 years.

You can get orders to Hawaii, signing a bonus of thousands of dollars, even a different MOS or college. He can also go to the Officers program and get paid to go to college. The military can be a very different experience the second time around. Don't be so quick to judge those who do re-enlist. If it were an easy choice to make, everyone would make the same one. It is not hard to *say* you will never re-enlist. I too, once said the same thing, although my husband and I have considered re-enlistment several times and it is still a very real possibility. Whatever you do, it is a brave decision. Choices are harder to make when you face them in real life.

Q & A

Q. My husband was supposed to get a weekend pass, so I bought a ticket. Now, they have revoked his pass!

A Yep . . . that's what they do.

Q. I will absolutely DIE if we get stationed there!

A. Start making funeral arrangements, you have just broken a cardinal rule. Never *ever* plan on things going your way. The military will never do the rational or appropriate thing and they don't care about your hang-ups about it. Q. How often do passes and 96s come?

A. "Ninty-six equals hours. They usually happen on national holidays, like Labor Day weekends and such. However, they can be revoked, so don't count on that time. In fact, don't count on anything!

Q. My husband says that he is owned by the Army. How can anyone like that kind of life? Not only like it, but love it?

A. It is a wonderful thing to be controlled . . . why did you think he got married anyway?

CHAPTER 10

Kissing Him Goodbye (Deployments)

My Husband, the Killer

This is a hard concept for me to accept, but most wives never think about it. While I watch my husband playing kissy-face with my daughter, it is hard to think that he may someday be taken away from me. But who would take him away for good? Certainly, not the military. I don't think they have resorted to executing their own soldiers yet.

The most probable answer is that the "bad guy" would kill him. My poor husband would be killed by the "bad guy" while he was just trying to do his job . . . kill the bad guy. This is why I think war is stupid. I have never met a soldier, Marine, airman or seaman who really *wanted* to go to war and fight and kill someone. I really have trouble believing that the "bad guys" are so much different in general.

Of course, I prefer my husband to come home, as opposed to the bad guy. But even if the other side is not so innocent, do they not have a wife and children at home, too? I mean, it's not like they hate us anymore than we hate them—they are just doing their job, too. It is a difficult and emotional concept with many sides.

Wars should stay where they begin, in the Congress and the White House. Leave it to the president to figure it out. I mean, isn't that why they pay him the big bucks? So if war was to stay in the White House and in the bigwigs' offices, we would have a national and worldwide interest.

Imagine it on pay-per-view tonight! "In the left corner, representing America, the president of the United States, George Bush!" [Cheering from large audience in boxing arena] "And, in the right corner, representing terrorists of all ages, all the way from the Middle East, Saddam Hussein!"

The leaders of the war could fight their own battles and leave us decent citizens with families out of it! Let them fight to the death, I would pay to watch it, as would many other sports enthusiasts. If our president lost, I think it would be prudent to nominate someone bigger, like a professional sumo wrestler. Sure, he may not be made in the U.S.A., but I would allow him to defend it.

Of course, none of this will ever happen, and mentioning the president in reference to a fight to the death is probably unbecoming of a military wife. However, why don't we elect cool guys to the office? Maybe, teenagers should be allowed to vote so that we could elect based on pure looks and popularity, instead of politics. Let's make America a little more entertaining in our generation!

But until the day the government starts listening to my brilliant pearls of wisdom, we will continue deploying military men. I have learned that the military changes you—you don't change the military. So many women, and no doubt you too, feel that they cannot deal with a long separation. Everybody feels that way. But it can, and will be, endured. So brace yourself and be prepared, a deployment is inevitable.

Checklist for Deployments

* You have a current Power of Attorney that will not expire until he returns* You know how to obtain a copy of his LES at www.dfas.mil, and you have his password for doing so.
* You have a pre-arranged amount of money that he can take from the checking account or other arrangements for him to acquire money while he is away. (You must both understand and agree to the terms before he leaves!)

* He has "briefed" your children on where he is going and why, and has reminded them that he loves them and that he will be back.

* You have the phone number to the command or another emergency contact number in case you have a problem. It is also helpful to have the number of Red Cross and know the procedures for sending a message.

* You have arranged for someone to check up on you at least weekly, such as a friend or family member.

* He has taken care of any military paperwork and allotments.

* He has called all of his family to inform them he will be leaving—you do not want to be the one telling them after the fact.

* He knows how to get hold of you based on your schedule. (E.g., you will be at your parents', visiting for a month, etc.) He has the numbers to your family members' homes where you may be staying at, and a local contact number for one of your friends or family members who can check on you if needed.

* He has a phone card. Preferably, one that works overseas.

* You have his family's phone numbers and know whom to contact in case of an emergency.

* His family has your number, and also knows how to reach you in case of an emergency.

* He has checked the car to be sure that it is in tip-top condition. It will never break down, until he is not around. He has also given you the numbers to his mechanic (hopefully one who will not rip you off) and checked the tires for you. It may also be a good time to put a first aid kit and flashlight in your car, sign up for triple A, or get a cell phone, in case of roadside emergency.

* You know what is and is not allowed in care packages based on the command, his circumstances, and the country he will be in. (Some countries consider *Maxim* magazine pornographic and therefore, it is illegal.) You have the

address where his mail can be sent, or know that you will
get it soon after he leaves.
* Your name is on all of your utility accounts. Some of them
will not speak with you if your name is not on the account,
and they don't care where he is.
* He has checked the smoke detectors and air filters in your
home and taught you how to perform emergency house
maintenance, such as lighting a pilot light.
* You have given a trustworthy neighbor a set of spare keys in
case you get locked out.

Remember that your main concern with deployments is about
your day-to-day problems. He should take care of everything he
can for you before he leaves. Who will be mowing the lawn, stopping
that allotment, making appointments with transportation?
Anything that he does not take care of before leaving will become
your responsibility. Prepare accordingly.

Selfish Wife Syndrome: This Is Going to Suck for *Me*.

I hear so many wives complaining about how horrible they
will feel (or have felt) while their husbands are deployed. It seems
to me that oftentimes, we are very selfish. We very rarely think or
talk about what *he* will be going through during this deployment
phase. But when you do think about it, you may realize that you
are neglecting to think about his feelings.

He will be leaving his wife and child(ren), whom he loves very
much, alone to fend for themselves. He may worry about his wife
cheating, just as you may worry about his fidelity. He will be
living in a tent/ship/barracks (instead of his comfy home) with at
least 2-3 other men and eating MREs. He will be without his
trusty TV remote and favorite pillow, and every other comfort of
home.

You, his wife, will be here missing him, spending time with
the kids (whom he misses) and going on with business as usual in
the comfort of his home. Although you are going through a

separation, he is going through a much more difficult change involving his entire life. On top of that, you have time to yourself, the family car to yourself, and you will probably be going to visit relatives if he is going to be gone for any significant period of time. Sounds like a good vacation to me, and probably to him, too.

As wives, we should think about our husband's feelings more often. Perhaps, he needs reassurance from you, rather than your complaining about how bad things will be for you while he is away. Perhaps, he is tired of trying to be strong and listening to you whine. Perhaps, it is time for you to be the giver in the relationship and allow him the opportunity to be the taker.

Straighten Up!

Many husbands tend to pull away from their families before a long separation from them. This creates a major dilemma for the wives, who feel that they should be spending as much quality time together as possible and making memories for the upcoming deployments. I tend to agree with the women myself, but I may be biased.

Many times, this occurs because men don't know how to express their feelings like women do. They are emotional idiots. Therein lies the conflict of marriage in general. Emotional stupidity is just something you are going to have to deal with if you want to have a man in your life.

The best approach I have found to solving this problem is to confront it. It will be much easier to do while he is around rather than over the phone during a five-minute (delayed) overseas phone call. Miscommunication is a difficult issue to face in person so you don't want to confront it while he is halfway across the world.

I find that the "Hey, straighten up and stop acting like an ass!" approach works best. But you know your husband better than anyone. Whatever you do, make sure neither of you feels bad about things before he leaves. If it's unavoidable, at least talk about it beforehand and make some sort of agreement or arrangement about how you are going to solve it in the future.

All in all, these separations can actually improve and renew your relationship. Deployments are a fabulous opportunity, if you *allow* them to be. How many spouses who aren't in the military write each other love letters and send care packages to each other after ten years of marriage? You have a unique relationship that can be used to your advantage if you are willing to approach it with the right attitude. Finding that attitude is up to you.

The Feared Long-Distance Relationship

Many women have posed the question of how to keep a long-distance relationship going in the military. Unfortunately, there is no real advice about this. Long-distance relationships are difficult in normal cases, but in the case of the military, they are almost impossible. This is why many couples choose to marry and live together rather than attempt many years of separation.

Unfortunately, even as a wife, you will have to endure periods of "long-distance relationshipping." I have found that this is not too hard, as long as you both care about each other as much as you say you do. A long-distance relationship is what you both make of it. That is all.

Making Due without Him: Getting You through It

I have heard a lot of people say a lot of things about military wives. How we have "courage" because we can watch our men leave us. This is a myth as far as I am concerned. We don't have courage because our husbands leave; courage is defined as encountering danger without feeling fear. I don't think I have ever watched a military wife send her husband off without fear.

I would like to hear from now on that we are reluctant, yet prepared for such an occasion—because it's the real truth. I personally try to avoid sending my husband to hostile countries, yet I know it is always a possibility. I do not, however, do it courageously. He does. He is the brave one. I am the one left behind while he pursues his military dream of becoming GI Joe.

As far as having "the strength to survive while he is away," there are many people who just aren't cut out for the military. However, not many women are completely incapable of functioning while her husband is away. Sure, it's hard to get out of bed sometimes, but let's give ourselves some credit here! We are not helpless individuals, and I assure you no one has ever died of being terribly lonesome while her husband was deployed for a few months (or even a year).

You have to be strong, and this is what makes you strong! This is also a fabulous time to travel and visit family, or take that college course you have wanted to take for so long. Your husband is sucking it up, eating MREs and sleeping in a tent, while here you are with the world at your front door, ready for you to conquer and no one to hold you back.

Strength is not just an advantage; it is necessary. If things ever seem to go wrong, they seem to do so while your husband is deployed. Your children and family members will likely need your support more than ever. When you are in an airplane emergency, you are instructed to put your mask on before attempting to assist others. You are useless to others (including him) if you do not help yourself first!

All women have the ability to be strong and I would like to see less of them locking themselves up in the house because their husbands are away. I have found that there are many things you can do that are impossible while your husband is home. Here are some suggestions:

* Have a slumber party with your girlfriends! Don't have any friends yet? Find out who else on this deployment has a wife at home, and invite them out to dinner. You will have many things to talk about.
* Go for midnight drives just for the hell of it.
* Just stop shaving, what's the point?
* Go out to dinner by yourself and be proud! There is no one there to argue with you about what restaurant you should go to.
* Read books, God knows you can't while you have a husband to amuse.

* Go shopping for care package junk! It's always fun to get to the local Wal-Mart and he will love it that you are thinking of him.

* Start taking yoga or karate and fantasize about how you will astound your husband with your new flexibility.

* Start that diet you've been thinking about. It will be much easier now since you don't have that husband scarfing down ho-hos and cookies right in front of you.

* Buy yourself stuff. You are only budgeting for one now, I'm sure the grocery money can be raided with the diet and all.

* Go bungee jumping or do something else your sniffling baby of a solider is too scared to let you do. (Tip: Don't tell him until after you have done it.)

* Get a video camera and make him a home movie about your exciting life back on the mainland. Make sure and show him that you have taken over his job of sitting on the couch, scratching himself so that he knows all the important jobs are still being done.

* Start a project that you have wanted to do, but make sure you have enough time to finish it before he gets home.

* See what your bathroom wall looks like after you paint it bright pink. Experiment with other decorating ideas of this nature. With any luck, the house will be completely "feminized" by the time he returns.

* Go out for a night on the town with the girls. If men hit on you, reject them and then start exaggerating about how great your husband is. They'll be out of your hair in no time.

* Write your husband a letter about the big tattoo you just got on your butt. Wait for his reaction by mail (it will be quite amusing). If you really did get a tattoo on your butt, wait until he gets home and surprise him with it.

* Make brownies, but eat all the butter and don't even bother cooking them. There is no one around to judge you.

* You can now safely leave all the lights in the house on and

no one will complain about the electric bill (except maybe you) at the end of the month.

* You can watch whatever you want on TV. No more sports, *Cops,* or *Real TV.*

* Watch some chick flicks and cry. Then discuss with your girlfriends how you can get your husbands to act more like the leading man.

* Stay up late.

* Discuss with your girlfriends all your husband's annoying little habits. You will definitely miss him less.

* Drive around on base looking suspicious; see how long it takes the MPs to ambush you.

* Drone incessantly to anyone who will listen about how your husband's branch of the service is the best. (You could probably do it while he is there, but he does it himself, so why bother?)

* Clean your house and notice that it takes a couple weeks for you to mess it up as badly as he does in one day. Write him a letter detailing such findings.

* Get on the Internet for hours . . . just surfing and being useless.

* Revel in the fact that you have 90 fun-filled days left where you don't have to iron cammies!

* Call old friends and talk as loud as you want.

* Sleep in the middle of the bed. And hog the covers while you're at it; empty beds are a GREAT thing!

* Do whatever it is you like to do that your husband considers geeky, embarrassing, senseless or unproductive.

* Instead of counting the days, count the trash days or the paydays until he returns. The numbers are lower and it makes the time go by faster.

* Catch up on your letter-writing to old friends that you may have been too busy for while your husband was around.

* Write a novel.

* Work in the garden. If you don't have a garden, get a planter box for your porch, or at the least, a chia-pet.

* You would not believe how clean your house can be. Steam the carpets, rearrange furniture and organize your closets. This is both rewarding and time consuming.
* If you are consumed by loneliness, get a pet.
* Go to the craft store to get ideas for a project.
* If you are like me, you can get lost in the bookstore. Go there and kill a few hours.
* Go to the gym!
* Do girly things like facials, makeovers and do your nails.
* Enroll the kids in those swimming lessons you keep thinking about.
* Volunteer.
* Start a playgroup; this way, you can interact with other moms!
* Rent movies on rainy days and build forts in the living room with the kids.
* Catch up on all those cartoons your husband was too manly to watch with you.
* Start a scrapbook.
* Start an at-home business.
* Get a job.
* Start college.

There are thousands of things that you can do to occupy your time. Anything that you didn't have time for while your husband was around will do. Anything that you normally enjoy but are prevented from doing is great. Make a list, while your husband is around, of all the things you wish you could do. Pull it out when he leaves. If you are a creative person, you will find many things to occupy your time while he is away. Remember that bored people are bor*ing*. Give yourself something to talk about on those phone calls!

That Obnoxious News Junkie

We all go through a phase during deployments where we are absolutely glued to the TV set, watching the news. The news will become more important than life itself simply because there is a possibility that you will see something about your husband's deployment and maybe even (all fingers crossed!) your actual husband!

The military creates these monsters by limiting communications and information. There will be weeks at a time when you hear nothing about him. Your phone will be silent for days and your life will become meaningless. You will X out each day on the calendar for what seems like an eternity, only to be disappointed day in and day out.

The smarter wives I have met are the ones who decided a long time ago that the news should be of no concern to them. I have adopted this theory and I am a much happier person because of it. If you want to be a happy person, don't watch the news and for your sake, don't cross days off on the calendar, counting down his return.

You can always find something bad in the news simply by turning it on. If your husband is home, he will watch the news and say "Oh shit, I must be going to the Middle East!" If your husband is in the Middle East and you watch the news, you think, "He's probably been killed out there! That's why he has not called me in three days!"

This kind of drama has no place in your life. It causes irrationality and hopelessness. These are two things that you (and everyone around you) is better off without. Believe me, you will annoy your neighbors if you throw yourself on the ground, blabbering uncontrollably over your husband's death—only to have him show up by surprise the next day. Your neighbors know that he only has one life, trust me. Save yourself the embarrassment and change the channel when the news comes on.

The Date of Return

As I have said, counting down the days to your husband's return is just not functional. It keeps you in the house, a slave to the calendar, wishing every moment that he would just come home. Basically, putting your entire life on hold. It doesn't have to be that way. You do have a life, husband or no. The reason you cannot rely on a calendar is because the military uses estimates, not facts, to predict that day you have circled with a heart.

This brings me to truth #17: *An estimated date of arrival is a joke.* When your husband tells you that he should be returning on "May 23," this does not mean he will actually be home on May 23. This is very complicated military terminology that the government has been perfecting for years. I will tell you the actual meaning so that you will have no surprises come May 23.

Some military equivalent of a "middle manager" has made an "estimate" on how long what they are doing will take. True to military efficiency, he knows nothing about what they are doing and is probably using some inapplicable military equation to figure it out. Remember that he may also be a civilian and if so, he is, in fact, completely clueless all together. After days of deliberation at the cost of several thousand dollars, the equation is complete: May 23. Either that or he just throws a dart at a calendar; it's about the same procedure as far as efficiency is concerned.

Either way, it is a highly tuned and expensive method of getting absolutely nothing accomplished. Remember that while you are still alone on your birthday, August 4. Maybe, you will get a good laugh out of it by then. As a good friend of mine once said, "The pretense of a schedule is scoff-able!"

Cockroaches

While my husband is on deployment, I take all the necessary safety precautions. I always lock the door. I don't give strangers information about my whereabouts over the phone and make every effort to make it appear as if he is home. But I am not overly concerned about it. I am a very independent person and I consider myself capable. Despite my constant efforts to ensure that there are no unknown persons invading my personal space, a few occasionally breach my tight security.

For those of you who are unfamiliar with overseas environments, it is pertinent that I inform you that household pests grow to a phenomenal size in the tropics. These hideous creatures cross the thin line that separates a mere bug from a mutated and unnatural bug. A flying roach once attacked me when I lived in Hawaii as a small child. Now, the sight of a cockroach still instills a debilitating and paralyzing fear in me.

I married with the assumption that my husband would be the primary bug killer in my home. However, since our marriage, I have discovered that not only is he a coward, he is a practicing bug rights activist. If a deadly rattlesnake slithered into my living room, he would refuse to kill it on the grounds that "it didn't do anything to us."

I still contend that any bug that enters my residence should be condemned to death for the breach of my personal territory. I find it humorous that my husband would have no problems killing a human intruder, but a harmless spider is too much for him to deal with. Maybe, we should get a gun to deal with these bugs.

I have dealt with every insect, from spiders to scorpions and even other pests such as mice. I still find it daunting to deal with a roach. I think that if I was confronted with a roach touching me, I might go into cardiac arrest and die. Who says they are harmless anyway?

That is why it is so amusing that somehow, these mindless insects can sense when my husband is absent. I have never seen a roach in my home while my husband was not on deployment. They dare to assault me with their presence because they are reassured that I am helpless to destroy them. I don't know who told them, but the secret is out and my number is up.

I beg of you to buy a can of bug spray before your husband departs. Either that, or have him bomb the house. Anything to avoid facing the sum of all your fears. Sitting on my couch with bug spray while watching TV, I can be confident that my borders will not be penetrated tonight. They dare not show themselves when I am prepared . . .

Whatever your fears may be, take care of them *before* your husband is gone. Make sure that you have all the necessary equipment to make you feel safe, be it breaking down on the side of the road or an attacker, the sum of all your fears will occur while your husband is helpless to protect you. Always take care of major concerns such as these and you will be glad you did in the event of such a trauma. Now, who will pick that dead roach up off the floor?

Happy Pills

Many women choose to use antidepressants, especially military wives, I've noticed. I believe that these drugs are overly prescribed. There is a difference between clinical depression and being depressed. I think what most military wives are experiencing is not clinical depression, but rather conditional depression or anxiety. Everyone feels sad while their husbands are away and they are left to hold down the fort with little human interaction and nothing to look forward to at the end of the day.

If you choose to use an antidepressant, I urge you to proceed with caution. Many people don't understand the nature of their own feelings, and I think that this is tragic. These drugs, widely referred to as "happy pills," seem to do just that. I think that they take away the very emotions that make you human. What you are going through while your husband is away is perfectly natural and you can find other ways to deal with it, short of drugs.

Try other things first. Go home and visit your family, or start going to club meetings, college, or get a job. If you keep yourself busy, you will be less inclined to feel bad about your life. If you feel that drugs are absolutely necessary, I recommend some short-term anti-anxiety drug such as Xanax. These drugs kick in faster than Prozac or Zoloft (which are meant for long-term use).

If you are completely unable to function without drugs because of debilitating long-term depression, stay on your medication. However, if you are not, consider carefully whether you are depressed because of the events in your life, or if you have a serious condition that requires long-term treatment. Then discuss these things with your doctor or choose to discuss them with your friends. Do not discuss them with your husband while he is overseas.

We all feel a little needy sometimes. It is unfortunate that we cannot always get the kind of support that we want, from the people we want. But that is why you must become resourceful and think smart and logically about things before you take action on anything. This is a major trait of a functional military wife and functional person in general. You are a capable human being, and you are strong. Keep in mind that your feelings are normal, and do what is necessary for you to overcome them.

Co-Dependent: Leave My Husband Alone!

My husband arrives home at about 8 P.M. after being called to work because someone dodged a urinalysis test. He already has 3 messages waiting for him, two of which are from wives. I don't know how they got our phone number, but I wish they would lose it. They have all called more than once and have been harassing me. Once again, I have left the answering machine to do the dirty work.

One woman's husband was deployed to Spain. He has been gone for one month. Maybe, there is some type of dementia that sets in while our husbands are away sometimes, I don't know. Apparently, it is my husband's job to keep these annoying women sane.

Her problem is that a Marine has threatened her. Instead of calling the police, she has chosen to call my husband and keep him on the phone for a full hour, telling him the story of how everything "went down" as well as "what's new in her life."

Is she a dependent wife? Not dependent enough on *her* husband, I think. My husband is polite. He calms her down and tells her not to be afraid. I am making faces and gesturing at him, trying to get the point across that he needs to get rid of her. He just shakes his head and continues with the conversation. He is a better person than I, obviously. I can hear her loud voice over the phone from across the room. "Oh, and the baby moved today! I want to tell Jim, but he has not called in a week . . . do you know why?" All very important information that I am sure could not have waited until tomorrow.

At 10 P.M., my husband has responded to all of his home messages, including the two "demented" wives. At this time, he lies down in bed and falls quickly to sleep. I now understand why he seldom answers the phone. These jabbering women seem to be stalking him, not to mention annoying me. The thought does not seem to register in their heads that *I* may want to spend some time with my husband before he is gone as well, or maybe they just don't care. In any case, *I* am not allowed to be selfish with my husband's time.

The military likes to say that they will be responsible for a wife while her husband is deployed. I tend to think of it differently. It does not take a village to raise a wife. My husband should be mine all the hours of his life he is not at work. Wives who hinder that are not independent, nor do I respect them. You must always think twice before you pick up the phone and disturb the family of another. Ask yourself if you are having a real emergency and if the problem could be better handled by another, or at least, at a more reasonable hour.

A month later, while my husband was deployed, I have a problem. As I pick up the phone to dial, I remember when these needy women stole time with my husband. It occurs to me that I should call their husbands and return the favor. I think better of it, though. My time is better spent productively. I am not just housewife, nor will I ever be. I am a military wife and I can handle anything on my own.

Getting the Kids through It

Many young men, upon entering the military, fail to understand or even think about how it will affect the lives of their wives or children. Many couples also fail to consider this when deciding to go career military, or at re-enlistment time, particularly if the child is very young.

As the men generally don't think about this, it is your responsibility as the wife to be conscious of it. Young children are, in fact, more able to deal with change as long as they are coached by their parents to have a healthy attitude about it. If you have an infant, you face bigger challenges than having a toddler, and if you have a teenager, you have got the work cut out for you.

If you have children, you will be a single parent while your husband is away. You will be of no use to the children if you are stir crazy. Get away from the kids once in a while so that you can blow off steam. As precious as they are, they are no substitute for the company of other adults.

Infants

Many infants forget their fathers during long periods of separation. I have seen children react badly to fathers, especially in cases where the child was born and turned six months old before he even met his father. This presents a challenge to the parents because the child may become particularly dependent on Mom for all caregiving (and still feel uncomfortable around Dad.) The child is learning that Dad is not around consistently, whereas Mom is. Mom is obviously more reliable.

You must consider your husband's feelings in regards to this. His ego will definitely be damaged when he holds his own child and she cries for Mom. To remedy this, talk about "Dad" frequently while he is away. Infants begin to understand language and feelings at a very early age.

You attitude will also affect your baby, so try and stay positive. If your husband will be gone for a long period of time, you might be going home. Make sure that there is another male around to keep the baby used to a man in the house. This may be a grandfather, uncle or even your husband's best friend from home. If you plan on staying where you are, ask a friend of his or one of your friend's husbands to play with the baby once in a while.

Never feel bad about leaving your baby with a baby-sitter. Actually, you should attempt to leave her with a baby-sitter frequently to let her know that even though you leave at times, you will always come back for her, and so will his dad. Make it a point when you are putting her down to say "Mommy loves you, and Daddy loves you too, and he misses you."

If you receive something in the mail from him, read it to the baby and show your excitement about getting "something from Daddy." Getting excited about the word "Dad" will get them excited when you say "Look, DAD!" Hold the phone to the baby's ear and let him talk to her when he is on the phone. This will help them both feel a little closer. Consider having your husband record his voice and play it for Baby while she is falling asleep. And if you have a video camera, you can play home movies for the child to help her remember her dad.

As I said, an infant is a difficult challenge. The biggest thing you have to worry about is the baby crying at the sight of her father. If you keep your infant used to having other people around, "sharing Mommy," and make it a practice to allow others to hold and play with him, the issue may be averted for your family or, at the least, downplayed. Eventually, your child will get old enough to understand some of what is really going on.

Babies are adaptable, and the biggest concern you should have about it is your husband's feelings. They will both get used to having each other around within a few days of his return, but it is up to your husband to begin bonding immediately. Fathers who remain withdrawn can cause a rift between father and child that sometimes lasts years.

Toddlers

A toddler presents less of a problem during separations, though they may not fully understand where Daddy is going. Have your husband explain to the child in advance where he is going and what he is going to do there. Give him a week or so to get used to the idea.

I have heard many stories about toddlers thinking that any man in uniform is their dad. If this happens, just calmly explain to the child that this is not their father, and *do not* tell your husband about it. This will make your husband feel bad, and I am sure he will miss the child terribly.

Make sure that you buy and send disposable cameras to/with your husband so that he can send back pictures of what he is doing. This will allow the child to feel more involved and remind him that his dad is gone because he has to work, not because he wants to be.

Before your husband leaves, get a project for them to do together and make special memories. An old favorite is making plaster molds of their hands. Both father and child can make one, but most importantly, father. This way, when the child feels lonesome, he can put his hand in his daddy's hand. This can also be done at care package time. On a piece of paper, have your child trace his hand and put it in the care package. Then when your husband receives it, he can trace his hand over the child's and send it back. Your child will get a kick out of "holding hands" with Daddy from so far away.

Furthermore, Dad can kiss the child's hand and explain to him that the kiss stays there. That way, when the child misses Dad he can kiss his hand or put it on a boo-boo and have a Daddy kiss. Either way, spending time with Dad before he leaves is important. Make sure your husband tells the child that he will always love him and miss him very much.

After your husband leaves, it is good to help the child put time into perspective. For instance, filling a jar with 180 pieces of candy and allowing them to eat one a day. When the candy is all gone, Daddy will be home. Also, you can make paper chains and allow the child to tear one off per day.

There are many creative ways of implementing this same technique and I trust that you can be creative for this purpose. Always allow the child to be involved in care packages. Tell your husband to send a letter or picture to the child every time he sends one for you so that he doesn't feel neglected. Also, continue the infant methods that I have previously mentioned.

If you are dealing with a particularly long deployment, putting the time into perspective will be a little harder. Get out your calendar and plan monthly activities; holidays work well. Place the calendar in a prominent place in your house like the kitchen. Count down to the activities, rather than the homecoming. For instance, December - Christmas; January - visiting grandparents; February - your birthday, etc. It is not necessary to plan an activity every month as long as there is something in the near future to count down and look forward to.

Focusing on getting your children through these hard times will help you get through them as well. Always keep in mind that your attitude affects your children as much as it affects you. If you are down, they will sense it and then they will be uneasy about it too. Staying strong and keeping your children active will not only pass the time for them - it will also pass time for you.

Getting Him through It: Care Packages

Care packages are one of my favorite parts of deployments. Don't ask me why, but I find shopping therapeutic. There are many personal things that can be included in a care package that you will find are practical for you and your husband. As I can only give suggestions, that's what I will do. For more care package suggestions visit www.geocities.com/militarycarepackages.

Food Items:
* Instant coffee. There are many flavored coffees that are very good.
* Powdered Gatorade. Send along a jug too.
* Powdered hot chocolate
* Kool-Aid (pre-sweetened, of course)
* Tea bags
* Slim Jims

* Crackers and Easy (spray) Cheese. Triscuits and Ritz crackers are great.
* Single servings of bagged chips. (The small bags stay fresh longer.)
* Candy, of course. (M & M's are great; hard candy - anything that won't melt.)
* Little Debbie snack cakes
* Bubble gum
* Snack mixes - Chex Mix, Gardetto's
* Rice Krispie Treats
* Applesauce, pudding or fruit cups with the pop-off lids. Send a couple of plastic spoons, too.
* Dry cereal. (The small, individual serving boxes stay very fresh.)
* Instant oatmeal or grits
* Pasta Anytime dinners
* Kraft Easy Mac
* Microwave popcorn

Fun Stuff:
* Send board games - the ones they have made into key chains.
* Videotape their favorite shows on TV.
* Send favorite magazines (his, not yours!).
* Get some white boxers and paint on handprints on the back and kisses all over.
* If they're gone over a holiday, do up one box with just holiday stuff. Be creative! Use streamers, confetti, balloons (not blown up), etc.
* Lots of disposable cameras. They can take pictures to send back to you!
* With a CD burner, make a CD of his favorite songs.
* Always write letters, but in addition, you might record your letters onto a tape.
* Send a few toys. Slinky, sidewalk chalk, squirt guns . . . anything extra silly.
* Send electronic games.

* Get a small baby food jar and fill it up with dirt from their back yard. You could also put sand from their favorite beach, with a shell inside. It's oddly comforting.
* Make a miniature scrapbook. Go to the craft store and get a small scrapbook (about 5"x7"). Get a few supplies and go crazy! Do a theme book - "A day in our lives" where you take pictures all in one day for the book.
* Blow up a balloon, but don't tie it. Holding it closed, use a permanent marker to write a saying or a short letter on the balloon. Deflate it and send with a note that says to blow it up.
* Books on tape are nice, or for an avid reader, send small paperback books that they can give away when they are done.
* If they're gone over their birthday, send a birthday box with streamers, hats, noise makers, a birthday card, and a birthday cookie decorated with icing (refer to the Tips section on how to ship cookies!). Record yourself and the kids singing "Happy Birthday."
* Foam footballs and basketballs, the miniature size. These will be used constantly!
* Very carefully open a box of Cracker Jacks and remove the prize. Put your own prize in the box (use the prize somewhere else in your care package). Put in a little note or a bigger prize. Then, carefully seal up the box so they don't see that you've tampered with it. Craft glue works best.

The Kids:
* Have the kids draw a picture or write a story every day. Put them all in a big envelope and send them with the care packages.
* Take video of the kids playing at the park, doing any school activities, or just sitting down and saying a personal message.
* Get some computer printer magnetic paper. Let the kids

use paint markers to draw a picture on it so the parent can easily hang it on the metal rack that they sleep in.

* Let the kids do their very own care package. Let them put in whatever they want.
* Use a casting kit to create a miniature plaster "sculpture" of a new baby's foot or hand.

Practical:
* Clorox wipes
* Baby wipes
* Razors, shaving cream
* Foot powder
* Shampoo, conditioner
* Aftershave lotion
* Soap or body wash
* Mouth wash
* Deodorant
* Laundry detergent, the kind you use at home
* Gel insoles
* T-shirts, underwear and socks, monthly.
* A big, fluffy towel.
* Eye drops, especially for those in the desert.

General Stuff:
* Send batteries. It sounds simple, but people forget.
* Sunblock
* A stress ball.
* Stamps, paper and envelopes with a nice writing pen might inspire a few more letters home.
* A padded mailing envelope, just in case they need to send home something they bought in port for you.
* Phone card (Try www.bigzoo.com for great rates!)
* Get some white boxers and paint on handprints on the back, kisses all over.
* With a CD burner, make a CD of favorite songs.

* Send at least a few very steamy letters. You can even go on-line and read sexy stories for inspiration, or copy them right into your letter!
* Wives or girlfriends can send sexy panties. Just be sure to put them in an envelope marked "private" so he won't open them in a common area and get embarrassed.
* If you use a particular scented lotion or if your perfume has a lotion that goes with it, put some in a travel lotion bottle so they'll always be able to have you close.
* If your special one is a reader, send a paperback book or magazine with love notes tucked at different places inside. They'll love finding the treasures as they read.
* Take a plain pillowcase of any light color. Using a contrasting darker color in fabric (or other washable) paint, make a "boob print!"

Missing Money

While my husband was on a 6-month deployment in Grenada, my parents bestowed upon me $1,000 as a gift. As my husband was absent and I had no immediate use for the money, I put it in my savings account and forgot about it. Several months later, as I checked the balance in my account, I was astounded to discover that all of my funds had disappeared. When I confronted my husband about this, he responded that he had taken money out of that account. When I told him how much was missing, he sheepishly replied, "I really spent that much?"

It is an age-old story. It seems to happen to at least one wife on every deployment and I have not run into one wife who has not experienced the "missing funds phenomenon" while her husband was away. It always happens once: ATMs malfunction, numbers are jumbled and the money is just gone. It can be anywhere from 50 to 2,000 dollars. Spent on anything his little heart desires.

The problem seems to be (largely) miscommunication. If you are lucky, he will have one ten-minute phone call per week. Hardly the time to discuss anything other than "I love you, I miss you, bye." You must be clear with your husband about how much money can be removed. No matter what emergency he may run into in the field, on the ship, or overseas, it is not nearly as important as the rent check. And you must make him understand this.

Many wives have tried unsuccessfully to deny their spouse money while he is gone. While this may seem like an easy solution, he will resent it when his friends are going out to drink and party. And if he has that ATM card or checkbook, he may just decide to take matters into his own hands and determine an allowance for himself.

I have found that rather than giving them nothing at all, what works best is to set up a predetermined allowance. Let's say $100 of every paycheck belongs to him to do with as he pleases. Have him take that money all out of the ATM machine once every payday. This will avoid forgetfulness regarding how much he has taken and save in foreign ATM charges.

If you find that this method does not work for yourself or your husband, it is time for you to confiscate his ATM card, until he can use it responsibly. Explain that although his happiness is important to you, you cannot allow him to fritter away your rent money while he is not there to remedy the problems he has created.

Instead, establish a separate account in his name. Every month, put his allowance into this account and leave it at that. It is his money and when it runs out, he cannot draw on the family account because you have taken his ATM card.

As I said, you should not be overly upset with your husband about this issue, unless he is genuinely not sorry about it. It seems to be a highly unconscious thing, like when you buy those expensive pair of shoes at the mall - even though you know you cannot afford them.

If he can steal money from his family with a clear conscience to purchase beer and cigarettes while he is away, I'd say it is time to get rid of him. That is more than a miscommunication or accident—it's ground for divorce. In most cases like this, it causes no serious harm and you will simply go without until payday. It's not pleasant, but it does build character.

Pictures from the War

There are many things you will find surprising about a deployment. For me, the pictures to home were always the greatest. As your husband leaves you, expect that he will be doing some complicated work out there. Until you get the pictures . . .

There he is, having the time of his life climbing Mt. Fuji, standing in front of a beautiful waterfall, in front of the Eiffel tower, and more! The even more interesting ones will come, him playing cards with the Afghan people, him slaughtering a donkey, or him on an airplane with his buddies holding up their weapons. And those smiles! Is he laughing? That bastard! Where does he get off having fun while you are here doing all the work?

Yep, it's a fact of life, girls, sorry. He will be having fun from time to time, sometimes, more than others. Evidentially, there are fringe benefits to being deployed. Did you expect him to send you pictures of him working? Who wants pictures of that? Many women snort and cavort about this, but I think it would be more fun to send pictures in return.

Do what you will while he is on deployment; no one is forcing you to stay at home pining away. Nay! Send him pictures of you visiting Niagara Falls or the White House. Tell him you showed the pictures of him "goofing off at work" to the president. Send a picture of you in his favorite chair with his remote with a nice "wish you were here" note. That'll show him.

There are many fun ideas to be had if you are creative. Just don't feel sorry for yourself. You can't blame him for accidentally seeing the world while he is overseas.

Choosing Your Words Wisely

No matter how angry you may be at your husband for any reason, save it! While he is on deployment (depending on his job), he will be risking his life and the lives of others on a daily basis. Like it or not, if he is feeling bad about anything personal, it will get in the way of his work.

When he is upset, he risks the lives of himself and others. While you may be angry, I'm sure you don't want him to be dead, and even if you do, you don't want the deaths of any innocent bystanders on your conscience. In other words, don't kill *my* husband!

I suggest getting a journal to write down all your pissy feelings, or just getting a good friend to act as a sounding board and reassure you that he really is a huge jerk. Always avoid saying or writing things like "I cannot handle anything without you here, and you don't care and neither do I anymore."

You know as well as everyone else that he did not choose his deployment, he only chose his job and he can't quit now just because you don't like it. Also, keep in mind that these unkind words will make him feel helpless and depressed and he may lash out. It doesn't matter if the world is falling down around you, save it until he gets home.

Another thing to avoid in letters or phone calls is telling him about feelings of depression. Saying things like "This is so shitty, I can't handle this on my own, you need to come home!" will not be helpful either. It is okay to say that you miss him, but leave it at that.

Telling him that you are depressed will get down his morale. Your job (as a loving and supportive wife) is to help boost his morale, not tear it down. Remember that he is the one doing the work out there while you are still in the comfort of your home. It doesn't matter how bad things get, wouldn't you rather be at home for them? Well, he isn't.

Quite a different situation can sometimes arise with your relationship if you realize a serious problem. Never, and I repeat, never tell him that you are leaving him, that you have met someone new, or anything else of this nature. You can save it until he gets home. If you have a conscience, you can be mature enough to tell him these kinds of things to his face, rather than on the phone or in a letter. The military will not stop because of relationship problems or any other problem for that matter.

If you don't hear from your husband for a really unreasonable amount of time (like 6 months or more), it is appropriate to call the command and find out what the deal is. Never make assumptions about what he is doing and why he is not writing or calling. These men can be pretty busy, and no matter what rumors you hear, most likely, he is too busy to communicate with you. If you assume (for instance) that he hates you and doesn't want to talk to you, you might feel pretty silly when he does call and has a perfectly reasonable excuse for not calling. In laymen's terms, don't believe a word you hear until you hear them from his mouth, or from the mouth of the president.

I realize that it is a huge challenge to maintain a meaningful relationship while separated for months at a time with little communication. I also know that it can be very hard to find something positive to say to a man whom you are so angry with you can barely stand it. And I know it is quite difficult not to be able to share your sadness with the man who is supposed to be your best friend.

But you must step back and look at the big picture and the things that are really important. The bottom line is, his life is more important than your petty arguing, sadness, or anger. All that matters is that he is returned to you safely. You can take the marriage stuff from there.

OH MY GOD! The Return

So the day has finally come. Your husband will be home in a few days. But there is a problem. You don't feel the way you thought you would. It has happened. You have become comfortable in your environment without him! Congratulations, you have survived the deployment functionally! You have adapted! Many women go through horrible anxiety before the long-awaited return of their husbands.

This can occur especially if you have gone through a major life change while he was away. Things like gaining weight, giving birth, or even becoming more independent are all reasons that make women feel nervous about the homecoming event. They worry that maybe, he won't find her attractive anymore, he won't like the baby, or there won't be anything for them to talk about.

This awkwardness they fear is usually baseless. I have heard of very few unsuccessful homecomings. While it may be strange for a moment, it does not take long to remember again why you love each other. He has been looking forward to this day as much (or more) than you have and he probably wouldn't care if you showed up wearing a garbage bag, so long as you were there to greet him.

In many cases, this leads to a renewed marriage. Everything about the relationship is new again - the stomach butterflies return and everything. It's great. You appreciate and love everything about each other and can even become downright obsessed.

Then in a couple of weeks, you will start to notice his annoying habits again, there is laundry on the floor and dishes in the sink. The honeymoon is over and everything is back to normal. All you ever wanted the whole time he was gone. Congratulations.

Remove Your Signs

You may notice while you are rolling into your first military base that there are signs of welcome hung out everywhere. God bless these creative women for some of these signs are so artistic and creative! However, among the fabulous artists, there are also several duds. Somehow, the duds always end up on the prime sign hanging real estate, while the more creative ones are stuck in corners and other hard-to-see places.

No doubt about it, the military town is certainly unique. You will notice these signs multiplying before a big deployment returns or a ship comes to port. The longer the separation, the more plentiful the signs. How exciting to be a young man returning to see all these creative (and not so creative) signs of welcome just for him!

After a while, though, they just look crummy. Deployments come and go and as life goes on, these signs persevere. Often made from a large sheet, the signs become weathered and old, ink runs and they are but a shadow of their former sign of glory.

It is obvious that the hanger got involved in other things after the welcome and never quite got around to removing them (especially the crummy ones). When your husband returns, you too may want to hang a sign. A proud remembrance to when your husband returned. A tribute, a memorial, if you will. Remaining for all time (at least, until the next wife wants your spot and decides to take it down). So save her the trouble, please take your signs down.

Q & A

Q. My husband tells me how hard he is working while on deployment, but every time I talk to him, it sounds like there is a frat party going on in the background. It is so frustrating! Why?

A. Your husband is working hard on deployment, just as he works hard on base while he is not deployed. However, almost every moment of his spare time (or at least, others around him) is spent doing frat-like and macho activities. To "relax." These activities keep morale high.

Q. I mean, it's wonderful having him back, but I'm not as excited about it as I thought I'd be. I'm just kind of exhausted.

A. Having a man around can be overwhelming at first, but you will adapt again.

Q. He just got deployed to the Middle East! I don't know what to do! He says "stay busy," but how can I do that when I won't see him until December?

A. You're right. Just don't do anything and stay miserable for the next 6 months. I hope he is dealing with the separation better than you are, or the country is in trouble.

Q. I am excited about the opportunity to travel. I like the idea of seeing the world WITH my husband. I abhor the idea of being on one side of the world while he is on the other.

A. Sounds like the Army is not for you.

Q. My husband has been deployed for a week now and I have not heard anything from him. Does he still love me?

A. Maybe not, I don't know you two real well . . . but there is also a possibility that during this huge movement of bodies, the military (in its infinite wisdom) has been unable to supply them with phone access. The military has been known not to foresee such foreseeable problems. But they will get around to it eventually. Bottom line: Just wait longer.

Q. My husband is currently deployed and I am pregnant. He is scheduled to come home soon, though. Should I be prepared to have this baby by myself?

A. YES. You should be prepared for anything! The military's official answer? "Maybe."

CHAPTER 11

Marriage and Family Concerns

Uncle Sam Wants YOU . . . to Be a Single Parent?

So, you think you want to have a baby? Perhaps, it will combat your loneliness while he is away. You might think that the military would offer a ton of help to support a baby. You get paid more for having a baby. Maybe, you just think babies are cute and want one of your own. Heck, having a baby seems to be the outright *smart* thing to do. As silly as this seems, I have met many women who rationalize it this way.

Before you have a child, there are many questions you need to ask yourself. "Do you make enough money?" "Will your marriage survive?" "Are you ready?" Another question that you must ask yourself (when your husband is in the military) is: "Do I want to be a single parent?" As unbelievable as you may think this is, you cannot count on your husband to be there for you, any more than your child can.

So you decide to do it - or maybe it's an accident. The bottom line is, you're pregnant. Not only do you have to worry about squeezing that kid's head out of (you know where), now you have to worry about your husband being there to witness the entire gruesome event. Furthermore, you must also be concerned about typical pregnancy things, like your baby's health, birth complications, etc. In addition, you may have concerns about the quality of care at your local military care facility.

After all this, you will have your baby. Maybe, your husband was in attendance at the birth, maybe, he wasn't. If he wasn't, you must now wonder what he will think of his new baby. What might he think of you while you are all post-partum-like? In the end, I am sure everything will work out.

Your very next obstacle is considering the stay-at-home-mom gig. No one ever thinks about what comes after all that pesky birth-giving stuff! But here you are, your husband is an E-2 in the Navy and you want to work. Well, did you want to get a night job? Keep in mind that good child care is expensive, usually as much or more than minimum wage. And you may have trouble trusting others with your new bundle of joy. If you get a night job, your husband can watch the child, but you will never have time to sleep.

The only other option (unless you have a good education and can afford the childcare) is to be a stay-at-home mom. Like many jobs, many people are simply not cut out for this job. However, many military wives end up being forced into it for lack of options. If you have little education and are young, you are "most military wives."

You may think that it's not a big deal to stay with this lovely child of yours all day long. But when your husband comes home, you may be in need of more stimulation than he can provide for you. You may want to go out since you have been in the house all day, and he could be too tired.

As soon as the weekend comes, he will want to go out and blow off steam with the guys or perform other non-baby-oriented tasks. This means that you will no longer be included in his social life. Not only will you not be included in his social life, you probably won't have one of your own either.

Contrary to popular belief, the higher-ranking your husband becomes, the less time he will have to spend at home. This means that your single parenthood will last for the remainder of his military career.

A baby will also restrict your relationship in other ways. You won't be able to just go see a movie or hang out with friends anymore. Hell, you probably won't even get to "just have sex" anymore. Every schedule you keep must be tailored to the child's schedule.

You already don't want the military controlling you; do you want a child controlling you also?

As if you didn't already have enough problems, a child complicates a marriage as well. If you have been married less than 2 years, I recommend waiting until you can be sure your marriage will last. You really have no way of knowing. No one gets married and plans for a divorce. And the military has an exorbitant divorce rate. Of the four couples I knew at our first duty station, three of them were divorced in the short couple years we were there.

Think it over very carefully. You will be trading a lot for this baby you want so badly. How will you feel while your husband is deployed and you become the child's primary caregiver? How will you feel while he is calling you from deployment, asking for more money to go to the bar with the guys, while you sit at home watching *ER* religiously?

Of course, there are ways for you to get a day off now and then and go out with the girls (or your husband). These times will be few and far between, but I promise you will not take them for granted. Motherhood has its rewards, like everything else, but you need to be sure that you are willing to give up the luxury of a partner who will help you.

And keep in mind that not only is the military taking away your child's father, they are also taking away his rights during fatherhood. It is quite possible that he will miss the child's first steps, first words, or an infinite number of other "firsts." Do you want your husband to be absent during those things? If he plans to get out, it might be the best for all concerned to wait to have a baby.

Thinking It Over . . .

Family is a big commitment in my book. I see women committing so quickly, without a second thought to what they are doing. Although many people think you should have kids while in the service to avoid paying the cost of childbirth, this will not save you from the cost of a child. I don't believe you should have children while you are in the military at all, especially if you are young and enlisted. As an afterthought, having a child is a struggle up until at least E-5.

Although I had my first child while my husband and I were both young and he was enlisted, I do not condone it. This is because it was a *constant* struggle. Many young wives have children to make up for things that they don't like in their lives. No one ever thinks that a child at this time in their life would put all things on hold, including college. And as much as most people (and wives) hate the military, children are one of the best reasons people have for re-enlisting.

Like it or not, an enlisted man usually possesses no marketable skills that are useful in the civilian job market. Although my husband was a superior Marine Corps engineer, he could not be employed as a civilian because he lacked the basic requirement - a diploma. As sad and unfair as this is, it's how the world works. And when that serviceman discovers that there is nothing in the real world that will give military benefits so readily, re-enlistment seems like the only option. Those children whom the couple wanted so badly often serve as the sole reason husbands end up prolonging their enlistment, even when they don't want to.

If you are both planning on going career military (or he has already been through college), and you don't have any plans to go do anything else with yourself, then I would say go for it. There is nothing wrong with raising children in a military family; it builds character and teaches them independence and pride at a young age. Just be sure that you know you will remain with this man forever. The last thing you want to be is a single mother, with no job skills or money. Trust me, his child support will not support the livelihood of you or your child. I know, however, that my words will be in vain. If a child is your dream, go ahead and pursue it. I know that my warnings bear no real weight in the matter anyhow.

Please seriously consider your plans for the future before making any expensive life choices like these. If you can't afford something or you don't know if you will be able to afford it in the future, it is probably best to wait. That goes for all expenses. However, there are not many other expenses that you can get quite as attached to as a child.

Adoption and Infertility (After You Have Thought It Over!)

Women who are unable to conceive are benefited by the military. TRICARE will help immensely by paying for infertility treatment and other things of that nature. Once the kid comes out, though, you are pretty much on your own!

. The military will also help with adoption costs up to $2,000. Contact your local JAG office for more information. Bear in mind that if you do begin the process of adoption and you are re-stationed in the middle of it, you will be forced to start over at your new duty station. Sometimes, this can crush your spirit more than not having a child at all.

As far as dependent pay goes, you will be getting paid a few dollars more for your child, but not a significant amount. Most lower-ranking enlisted men qualify for such programs as WIC and Food Stamps. If you are having problems paying to raise a child you already have, these things could become necessary. If you cannot compose yourself during a deployment, you will have an even harder time while you are pregnant or with a small child.

Your Military Brats

No matter what it is you dislike about the area you live in, your kids will adapt. Not only will they adapt, they will most likely pick up a few things in the process. For instance, in Hawaii, it is a custom to remove your shoes before entering a house. I just quit wearing shoes when I was a child. On top of that, I picked up the local slang.

Imagine my surprise when, as a seven-year-old, we went to Ft. Sam Houston. Texas is also a different kind of place to live. But I was often different there after being in Hawaii. When I went into second grade, the school wanted to check my head for "lice." "What's a vice?" The school nurse got frustrated with me as she explained the meaning of the foreign (to me) word. "Oh, you mean *Okus*! Okay." My mother received a call that night from the school nurse, who was concerned about my vocabulary.

I soon discarded the word *Okus* in Texas and picked up the phrase "y'all" instead. I was almost considered a local when I went to Ft. Hood, Texas. It was not long, however, before the other parents in my neighborhood discovered that we weren't Baptists and therefore, forbid their children to play with me. I remained friendless for a long time there and I never could understand why.

Moving to Ft. Benning proved to be not so bad, until I got to my first day of classes. It seemed that I was no longer a religious minority, but rather a racial minority. I was considered disrespectful because I was not in the habit of calling teachers "sir" and "ma'am." Male classmates harassed me. The principal told me I was "asking for it" and did nothing. Naturally, when a boy grabbed me between classes one day, I socked him. I probably would have been punished for that had he had the courage to tell on me. He didn't mess with me again after that, though.

Colorado was a bit more normal. Although now, I was no longer in a military town. I proved to be much more mature than many of the children my age. I was made fun of for calling my teachers "sir" or "ma'am." I got into countless fights because I had once lived in Hawaii. The other girls thought I was lying. Apparently, they believed that their small town was the center of the universe. I guess they never met an Army kid before. Maybe they never heard of the Army at all . . .

I faced diversity and hardship from the time I was very young. It seemed that every time I would adapt to my surroundings, the military would go changing things all around again. You will notice your children adapting. Kids are often cruel and it's a tough lesson to learn. Certain defense mechanisms will be evident.

Assist them in sorting out their problems through any way you can, and leave the learning up to them. But mostly, allow them room to grow. They are facing much greater hardships than you are, so you can learn from them, too.

Your Super-Sized Military Brat

Teenagers are a difficult part of life in general, as I understand it. As they are already old enough to understand and have probably been dealing with the military for a considerable amount of time anyhow, your biggest challenge is the moving.

Teenagers, even from military families, deal with a move considerably badly. At this time in life, friends are very important to them and their school is the foundation on which all life is built. These are the main things that a move will take away from them.

Being a military brat myself, I understand that a move represents not a mere hardship to a teenager, but a major life trauma. Uprooting is difficult for everyone involved, but it seems to be particularly catastrophic for a teenager. They will get over it . . . in time. Perhaps, not for a long time. They are much less forgiving than children.

Upon being notified of a move, you should immediately call a family meeting. You may have trouble explaining to your teenager that you have no choice in the matter and you cannot change it. But stand firm, it really is not your fault. But keeping them out of the loop about a move is not sparing their feelings, it is sparing your own feelings and taking from them their time to get used to the idea.

Try to stir up some excitement about the upcoming move. Find out about where you are going and what it's going to be like. Allow them to be involved in the move by telling them to pack their own room. Attempt to generate merriment during the trip by stopping frequently and treating your move like a family vacation. Once you arrive, allow your teen to pick his/her own room and let them participate in the house-hunting activities. If they have some input into their new home, it can soften the blow.

Before getting too upset about your brat's attitude, consider for a moment all the things he or she is missing out on. His childhood friend is probably long gone by now. He has never had that tree house in the back yard. He will graduate from high school with friends whom he has known for a year or two, rather than a lifetime. Everything a child normally associates with stability is missing for him. While his peers are still preparing to go see the world, he has seen it.

You probably find that your teenager loathes moves as well as the military, and maybe even you at times. I find this interesting as I had the same feelings as a teenager and swore I would never move after I turned 18. Most adult "military brats" that I meet today have trouble staying in the same place for more than a couple of years. People are creatures of habit, I guess. Military brats also have a tendency to be either shy or outgoing to an extreme. They may also develop problems with trust and sometimes, even forming long-term relationships is hard for them. There is no doubt in my mind that the military always leaves its mark on people, young or old.

Although your teenager may seem to have trouble adapting now, the moving does teach them to truly "grow where they are planted." In adulthood, anyhow, military brats are some of the finest and most interesting people I know. They come from many places and have experienced things that most adults never have to deal with. They are more mature and they seem to have a better understanding of the way the world works. They get along with people better, respond to criticism well, and can look at the big picture (when they are adults).

Though they may not participate in sports or other extra-curricular activities, they have spent their lives observing different cultures and people. They seem to be truly skilled in the ways of the world and react responsibly when faced with diversity. Chances are, people will like him/her everywhere he/she goes, and this is a skill that brings success. You are giving your child a gift by raising him/her in the military. He may think that it's unfair, but that is how the world is. And, after all, you are preparing him to go into the world.

When I was a child, the Army relocated me every year. I have lived everywhere from Hawaii to Georgia and I have seen and faced a lot of challenging situations. I have learned the local customs in

Hawaii, faced my fear of snakes in Texas, been the minority in Georgia, and been made fun of for being a military brat in Colorado. Was this easy? No, it wasn't, and I lashed out at my mother for it as a teenager.

However, now, I thank her for allowing me to have these learning experiences for they have made me who I am today. I never realized how much the Army taught me until I was an adult. I feel confident that if I can deal with the military as a child, I can deal with anything as an adult. And to this day, when someone asks me where I'm from, I say "the Army," because it's the truth.

The Exceptional Family Member Program

I once spoke to a woman whose husband had recently joined the Army. Although she seemed nice enough, she was incredibly diluted. She believed that her husband had joined under special circumstances because of her instability. Not only was she emotionally unbalanced, but she also had some sort of back injury that prevented her from moving around without a lot of pain. She also had a daughter who was about four years old.

She had explained to me that they had been living in utter poverty and that is why her husband had chosen to enlist. Her back injury, as well as her child, prevented her from working to contribute to the family funds. The medical bills had been piling up for quite some time. Somehow, they had ended up in a recruiter's office and it was obvious that they had been royally taken advantage of by some scummy recruiter. Either that, or she had only heard the things she *wanted* to hear from him, which is a possibility, given her incredible co-dependence and instability.

She said that as soon as her husband completed boot camp, he was going to enroll in the Exceptional Family Member Program (which they **did** qualify for) and he would be non-deployable. She went on to say that it is impossible for her to live day-to-day life without him. She could not ever handle him going to war or being sent anywhere else, and she fully expected that she would be staying put in her hometown.

As many times as I tried to burst her bubble about her delusion, she refused to hear me. She continued arguing with me that they had no other choice and she knew that they could not deploy him because she would die. Eventually, I had to stop talking because she wasn't listening anyway.

The Exceptional Family Member Program does exist. Although they will not put your husband on a non-deployable status because of any ailment you may have, they may change his duty station (a compassionate move) or get TRICARE to pay for a home nurse to care for you while he is away. They may also refrain from PCSing you so that you may stay in the same place as your doctors or specialist.

But if they decide that your husband is certifiably non-deployable, they will discharge him from the military without ceremony. They have no use for him if they cannot treat him like a soldier. The military does not do well with special cases.

I don't have anything but sympathy about this woman's situation, although I do feel quite annoyed by it at the same time. Obviously, she was quite unbalanced and it seems she will be heading for a breakdown the first time she discovers the real nature of the military. Her husband enlisted in the Army during a time of war and she had no idea what that meant. Perhaps, her husband will be discharged because of her condition. If she is so unstable, I hate to think that he would leave her alone for any period of time with a child in her care. But that won't solve any of their problems. A hardship discharge can take years.

If I learned anything from this woman, she just reaffirmed my beliefs about the military wife. I felt sorry for her, yet at the same time, appalled that she though she was so much more special than any other wife. I also feel happy that I am not so naúve and that I will never be disappointed so severely. Co-dependence is not my style, nor has it ever been.

When my husband is deployed, I will miss him, I will wish he was home, but I will never "die" because he is not there. I will never have a mental breakdown because the military acts like the military. I will never be disappointed because the military does not recognize that I should be an exception to the rules that govern *everyone* in it.

The reason why these things will never happen to me is because I won't allow them to happen to me. I choose to live my own life regardless of what the military dishes out. At the end of the day, when the military hands you lemons, you need to make some lemonade, or you are going to be up to your ass in lemons.

Prostitutes in Uniform

You will hear tons of things about the women who work with your husband. I don't know if wives are jealous or what. But I have heard a lot of things from my husband about these women also.

There are a few girls in my husband's company that seem to like being "slutty." I personally have no problems with this as long as they are engaging in these activities with unmarried men. You shouldn't either. One of these women cannot have sex with your husband without his permission, so don't worry about them.

These women are in the military for the same reasons many men join the military: college money, a job, honor, or to get out of their hometown. And suddenly, they are stereotyped by many wives as "husband thieves." I am sure that there are just as many or more civilian temptresses out there who would try and seduce your husband if he is willing. I am also sure I could find two slutty men in the barracks for every one slutty woman. Don't worry about this, it is energy better spent elsewhere.

If you want to worry about your husband cheating with someone, go to a bar in any military town. Sit far away and watch a married man try to have a beer by himself. Although surrounded by single servicemen, he will be flooded with women who want to take *him* home. These are the real "prostitutes" in the military, civilian singles in military towns.

I have always said that the single guys should be the ones wearing the wedding bands. It is an instant challenge to these women that is hard to resist, I suppose. In any case, if someone tries to seduce your husband, don't get too upset about it, unless she succeeds. And then, be upset with *him*. He is the one who is committed to you, not her.

My husband and I laugh about women who try to pick him up in bars all the time. You must have a sense of humor about these things or you will never survive. I mean, if you can't laugh about that, how will you ever laugh about any of the more serious things going on in the military?

Stupid Sgt. Smith

Twice in the past, my husband had covered duty for Cpl. Smith. Smith owed him in return for the favors. That's why when my husband had to be in Raleigh for a placement exam, he figured Smith would cover him. He called and let Smith's wife know the problems that he faced with duty. She assured him that Smith would call back.

A couple of hours later, he still had no response. The next morning after the duty had commenced, Smith called with a lame excuse about why he never called. The real excuse was that he did not want to stand duty. He could have said that, but he didn't. I guess he didn't want to look ungrateful.

A few weeks later, Smith picked up rank. He continued to disrespect his fellow Marines. No one took a liking to Sgt. Smith. It was not long after that when Smith lied about a weapon count report—to my husband. Tim, the trusting man that he is, failed to double-check. There were actually three weapons that were unaccounted for. That night, guess who got called back to the barracks to locate the surplus? It sure as hell wasn't Smith!

The very next day, Smith's name ended up on the duty roster. Thankfully, my husband had not paid dire consequences for the weapons mistake. However, Sgt. Smith (upon learning he was on the duty roster) promptly ordered my husband to take the duty for him. It was not a question - it was an order. He then stormed out of the room, angry about the show of disrespect that several Marines gave him that day.

Sgt. Smith didn't attend his duty and a Marine in the barracks was forced to pay for his absence. However, the next day, Sgt.

Smith pointed a finger at my husband. This time, it didn't fly. Whatever Sgt. Smith's consequences were, I'm sure they were far too lenient. Sgt. Smith was a bad Marine and he did not belong in the military brotherhood. Selfishness has little place here, and I pray that he is never covering my husband in any dangerous situation. He obviously cannot be trusted to do the right thing in the face of danger, or even discomfort.

My husband is a nice guy. Unfortunately, this is not to his advantage in the military. Nice guys finish last. Camaraderie is a great thing, but trust is often misplaced. Weather it be theft, backstabbing or recklessness, there are bad people everywhere and the military is no exception. The difference between the military and the civilian world is that there are a lot more opportunities to see a person's true color. You may not always like what you see. I have found it to be a fact that no good deed goes unpunished, no matter how pure the intentions behind it.

If you too are cursed with a husband who is a "good guy," odds are that you and he will be paying most of the consequences. You will be alone for that duty and you will be mad at the Sgt. Smiths of your world. You must maintain a good relationship with your husband, nevertheless. This kind of thing (as stupid and petty as it may be) is the kind of thing men and women fight about. I, too, am annoyed when my husband is too nice, but it's just not worth the fight. It won't make him act meaner to anyone, except to me.

Inalienable Truth That Can Hurt Your Family

Truth #18: *The military just loves to get involved!* I know it sounds great, doesn't it? What more could you possibly ask for in an employer? Let me tell you: a lot.

Just ask the military and they will tell you. They seem to think they have the answers to everything. Marriage problems? They have a guy for that! School problems? They have a program for that. Alcohol abuse problems? They've got *mandatory* counsel for that, too. Money problems? Oh . . . well, you are on your own with that one, but they are more than happy to tell you that you have too many bills and you need to pay them off. (Or risk their further meddling into your lives.)

Try not to discuss any kind of personal matters with anyone affiliated with the nosy government. It will end up in your husband's paperwork. Have you heard the phrase "loose lips sink ships"? So, too, can they sink your family while the military is attempting to "help" you.

And by the way, someone may call you when you arrive at your first base, inviting you to join their club. You may think it sounds like a good way to make friends. Well, not really.

In truth, many of the women who attend meetings like this turn out to be "crusty old wives" (read: nosy snitches). Not all of them, mind you, but you should trust no one at first. At least, not enough to start divulging personal information about your family that could be interpreted as dysfunctional in any way. And let's not pick bones here, every family has got its dysfunctions in one way or another.

Truth #19: *Nothing will ever be taken care of in a quick and timely fashion.* This may seem harmless enough on the outside, the old "hurry up and wait" joke. But when you look in your account and that money isn't there, it stops being so amusing. The finance office may tell you that the problem won't be fixed for 4-6 weeks, and you will not be paid until then. There is nothing funny about that, and it does hurt your family.

The only paperwork that is taken care of in any kind of quick fashion seems to be enlistment paperwork. Enlistment paperwork is effective immediately, unlike all other paperwork that can take up to 90 days (or longer) to take effect.

As much as wives like to think differently about this, I assure you it is the truth. Just ask a TRICARE representative when the (any kind of) paperwork will take effect after they receive it. He or she will then give you their full disclaimer of liability. Their general response is: "About 90 days." Of course, this is only an estimate. Some paperwork takes years. The more important the paperwork to you or your family's well-being, the longer it will take to process (if they don't lose it).

The military figures that as long as you still belong to them, they can take as long as they want to take care of you, the way your recruiter promised. And damn the consequences to you. Be sure and call the responsible party to show your gratitude if your important paperwork takes less than 90 days to process. (Try to encourage the good work, you will seldom see it.)

Things No One Ever Tells You

*   Payday weekend is the worst on the base; try and avoid the crowds, if possible.
*   Your husband is subject to random drug testing.
*   Military towns undergo a complete exodus in the summertime. If you are not moving, all your neighbors will be.
*   Bases are loud. If you live near the base, your nights and weekends will be interrupted by helicopter flyovers, random alarms, and the sound of constant gunfire. If you choose to live off-base, living a few miles away is nice.
*   Cell phones get military families in trouble. Your family probably has no need for them, if you can avoid it.
*   Military chaplains are people too. There are good ones and there are bad ones. Be sure and talk to one a few times and ask them about what he is required to share with the military before you open up to him or her.
*   The Geneva Convention: We seem to be the only ones who follow it!
*   All the buildings on post are numbered. They will be called by their numbers. Unlike regular street addresses, these numbers are in no logical order. If you are trying to find building 400, just ask for directions. Bases are very large and easy to get lost on.

CHAPTER 12

Final Last Words . . .

Getting Out

My husband is now two days away from his discharge date. It seems that the military is not without a sense of humor. In any situation, the military has never failed to put me in my place and has never missed an opportunity to teach me another lesson in life.

They have just informed my husband that he is being affected by a Stop Loss law, enacted by George Bush. Coincidentally, our president signed this law the day of his scheduled discharge. Adding insult to injury, we also have not been paid. Next week will find me in Orlando, Florida, on our "getting out of the Marines relaxation vacation." I will, however, be alone on this trip.

As if I hadn't learned this lesson enough times, the military has had the divine wisdom to remind me once again of it, so that I could remind you. The lesson? You just can plan for anything. While this is true in any walk of life, it is painfully true in the military. I know my husband will get his discharge someday. But at this time, that day will remain a mystery to everyone, including the military.

Never fail to recognize truth #20: *Expect the unexpected.* It is inevitable. Just when you think that there is nothing anyone can do to make your situation more joyful or more miserable, someone will. That someone is usually the military. They could ruin a wet dream.

If this comes as a surprise to you (as it did me), you may look or feel foolish. It is best to think of the military as your nemesis.

Treat them (and think of them) as you would any bully. Try to ignore them and never let on that they are bothering you. Eventually, they will get bored and leave you alone (in 4 years, or in my case, a bit longer).

Active Reserves

All the people I have ever spoken to in the active reserves tend to anger me. During the Gulf War, there were thousands of families living in utter poverty because the active reserves had been called. Businesses went under, houses were repossessed, and everyone bitched about it. They started donations for these poor families that were left alone with no money while their husbands and fathers were sent away to do their part in the war.

Never mind the active duty families that are always in dire straights and are being deployed even when not in time of war. I don't hear them complain much. You know why? Because we understand that this is what we signed up for! I have no tolerance for people knocking on my door, asking for donations to the reserves while my husband is deployed the same as they are. It's like asking the homeless to give to the poor.

It would not have bothered me so much if these people truly were victims. But they aren't. It does not take a genius to figure out that if you cannot survive on a salary less than $60,000, you cannot possibly afford to be called a reserve. This being the case, these men should not have been in the reserves, bottom line. Someone in these families should have known better.

I will never allow my husband to do this unless I am sure that we can afford to continue living if he gets called. That is the first question I ask myself before we commit to any life change: Can we afford it? If the answer is no, then we don't do it. If your husband is considering this, please think it through with the calculator first.

By the way, your husband will be inactive reserves anyway (after his first enlistment) if he gets out. Please keep this in mind even though it is highly unlikely that he will be called. It is always good to have a backup plan with any family member in any branch or status in the military. This is a good lesson from the military about being prepared. Hint: Now is the time to get prepared.

Separating

Many women complain about the military's many uncertainties. Yet, while my husband is currently checking out and on his way to separation from the military, I am living in fear of being a civilian again. It is something that you will never clearly understand, until your time comes.

Six months out from his EAS (End of Active Service) and I could not sleep or eat. He is having trouble finding a civilian job that will pay as much as we are making now. After working his way up, he will be starting at the bottom once again. We will have no health care. We have very little savings. We are enduring a move. For all the complaining people do about the military being "unstable," it seems that we are losing a lot of our stability here! And, at the moment, re-enlistment seems to be the easiest solution to a difficult situation.

Can he get out of the military and survive? Yes, definitely. I have seen it done on many occasions. Will it be easy? No. Depending on his MOS and schooling, there may be no jobs out there for him that do not require degrees. Therefore, he may not be able to continue working on the skill he has been perfecting for the last 4 years.

It is times like this when I wish we had decided upon our life plan *before* having a child. Without her, I would be confident in sending him to school on his GI Bill, but the current world makes that almost impossible and just too risky to endure with a child in our care.

All spouses and servicemen experience similar fears and uncertainties when separating from the military. You will probably be no exception, no matter what you may be feeling at this time. It is something that becomes such a big part of your lives that (after a while) you don't ever consider what life might be like without it anymore. And, although his enlistment has been wrought with problems, I wouldn't change a moment of it. When I look back on it, we were happy—and that is all that matters (or ever did matter.)

An Afterthought

Truth #21: *The military is the military.* Never doubt that. Trying to make yourself special by using the phrase "We are in the Air Force [or any other service or situation] so it is not the same" is a cop-out. If you don't think that any of the preceding rules apply to you because of whatever reason, you are still in for quite a few military bombings that will interrupt your life. You are in for a rude awakening when you actually encounter some of these things.

I have said it once and I have said it a million times: The military is the military, and that goes for *every* force. All branches are run by the same government, with the same laws and politics. Believe it or not, every branch has a few morons upstairs, like any other organization.

So what is the difference? *You* are the difference. Your husband is the difference. Your attitude, the way you chose to live your life and the way you chose to deal with the many bombs that will inevitably be dropped into your life without permission or warning.

Unfortunately, upon entering the military, almost everyone believes that they are an exception. You will learn sooner or later that the military simply does not play favorites. They don't care enough, at least, not in the lower ranks.

How can we change the military's attitude towards families? By giving them better families and stronger wives. By *not* living up to the military wife stereotype. Tragically, the military does not take responsibility for giving you the tools and information you need to become a success; they have left it up to you. Now that you have the information, it is up to you to gather all of your personal strength in order to endure for the next few years.

I would like to thank your husband for serving our country. I would also like to extend to you my personal regards and thanks in advance for attempting to become the best military wife the Army/Navy/Marines/Air Force or Coast Guard has ever seen. Good luck with all your endeavors and God bless all military wives, for it has got to be the toughest job I have ever taken so much pleasure in.

Visit our website for helpful links, advice or military wives support! www.SoloOps.com

Do you have a story you would like to share? Please direct all comments and inquiries to:

5023 W. 120th Ave. #187
Broomfield, CO. 80020